The Imagineering Pyramid

Using Disney Theme Park Design
Principles to Develop and
Promote Your Creative Ideas

Louis J. Prosperi

Foreword by Jeffrey A. Barnes, Ph.D.

Theme Park Press
www.ThemeParkPress.com

Praise for
The Imagineering Pyramid

"The Imagineering Pyramid decodes the mysteries of one of the most prolifically creative teams in business: Disney Imagineers. Better still, Lou Prosperi shows you how you can apply these innovative techniques to your own business ... even if you don't build theme park rides."

— David Burkus, *The Myths of Creativity*

"Walt Disney is a name synonymous with imagination, attention to detail, and above all, fun. Disney called his signature blend of creativity and technical excellence 'Imagineering'. Now *The Imagineering Pyramid* will teach you how to take the principles that built an entertainment empire and put them into practice in your work and life."

— Daniel H. Pink, *Drive* and *To Sell Is Human*

"The principles of themed entertainment design have been slowly making their way out of the park and into the 'real world' for several decades, and now Lou Prosperi has collected some of the industry's most enduring tenets and adapted them into real-world applications that can enhance both your personal and professional lives. His book is accessible and relatable, and I found myself looking at what we do for a living in fresh new ways that can live beyond the park."

— Jason Surrell, Creative Director, NBCUniversal

"Set aside the Tinkerbell dust to dig into the hard truths of creativity. Prosperi provides an E-ticket to the nitty gritty of what truly matters in business and the arts—execution."

— Robin D. Laws, *Hamlet's Hit Points*

"Are you the type of person who walks through a Disney theme park and you start to look at each element in detail, trying to figure out how they all add up to something wonderful? Yeah, me too. Lou is one of us. What he has done is to create a simple system to pull apart the complexity that surrounds you. I guarantee your imagination will be unleashed and you will not look at the parks the same way again. And that is a good thing."

— Sam Gennawey, *Walt Disney and the Promise of Progress City*

"I wish I had this book 30 years ago. A great creative process, well explained and useful for any endeavor. A must read."

— Sam Lewis, Senior System Designer

"Into the sea of creativity books, Lou Prosperi has thrown a much-needed life raft for everyone. *The Imagineering Pyramid* could also be called "Practical Magic". As a former Disney Imagineer, I can attest that Prosperi has captured the techniques and principles of Imagineers and crafted a fascinating, delight-filled, and useful look inside Walt's "sandbox". Keep it on your desk to implement these principles frequently. It's your turn to make some magic ... now!"

— C. McNair Wilson, former Disney Imagineer and author of
HATCH!: Brainstorming Secrets of A Theme Park Designer

"The genius of Walt Disney was his incredible and unique ability to have an idea, see the big picture, visualize the end product, and personally guide a team to accomplish that goal. Walt was a great casting director. We were cartoonists, animators, writers, and engineers that he brought together to become, what we now know as, 'Imagineers'. *The Imagineering Pyramid* takes Walt's formula and philosophy to the next level and becomes an in-depth journey through the creative process."

— Rolly Crump, former Disney Imagineer

"Collaborative creativity is a key component of modern business. In this book, Lou Prosperi presents a framework to help focus a team on their creative best for a project. Drawing upon examples from theme park attractions, game design, and instructional design, *The Imagineering Pyramid* illuminates a proven, scalable approach to team creativity."

— Greg Gorden, Game Designer

"Lou Prosperi loves Disney in a way that a special few understand, and he's taken that love and transformed it into an exceptionally useful book that will help you in any creative endeavor. I suspect this one will go right on your "Must Read" shelf alongside Ed Catmull's *Creativity, Inc.*"

— Sean Patrick Fannon, Pinnacle Entertainment
Brand Manager & Lead Designer, *Savage Rifts*

"Having been an Imagineer and Disney cast member for half my life, I could relate to all the principles that Lou wrote about in this book because I used them daily. What was brilliant, though, was how he found a way to apply many, if not all of the principles which were originally developed for use in the creation of Disney theme parks, resorts, cruise ships and other entertainment venues to work in any business model. With his clear and direct style of writing, he makes it easily understandable and fun at the same time."

— Louis L. Lemoine, former Disney Imagineer
and recipient of the Disney Legacy Award

In memory of my father, Harry Prosperi

When I was growing up, I never thought you understood me or my over-active imagination.

Riding Space Mountain with me at Walt Disney World showed me that you knew me far better than I thought.

Miss you, bub.

© 2016 Louis J. Prosperi

No part of this publication may be reproduced, distributed, or transmitted in any form or by any means, including photocopying, recording, or other electronic or mechanical methods, without the prior written permission of the publisher, except for brief quotations embodied in critical reviews and certain other noncommercial uses permitted by copyright law.

Although every precaution has been taken to verify the accuracy of the information contained herein, no responsibility is assumed for any errors or omissions, and no liability is assumed for damages that may result from the use of this information.

Theme Park Press is not associated with the Walt Disney Company.

The views expressed in this book are those of the author and do not necessarily reflect the views of Theme Park Press.

Theme Park Press publishes its books in a variety of print and electronic formats. Some content that appears in one format may not appear in another.

Editor: Bob McLain
Layout: Artisanal Text

ISBN 978-1-941500-96-5
Printed in the United States of America

Theme Park Press | www.ThemeParkPress.com
Address queries to bob@themeparkpress.com

Contents

Foreword ix
Preface xi
Introduction xvii

PART ONE:
Pre-Show: Peeking Over the Berm 1

  1   What is Imagineering? 3
  2   A Quick Look at the Pyramid 9
  3   Imagineering and the Power of Vision 13

PART TWO:
The Imagineering Pyramid 15

  4   The Art of the Show 17
  5   It All Begins with a Story 21
  6   Creative Intent 27
  7   Attention to Detail 35
  8   Theming 41
  9   Long, Medium, and Close Shots 47
 10   Wienies 53
 11   Transitions 59
 12   Storyboards 63
 13   Pre-Shows and Post-Shows 67
 14   Forced Perspective 73
 15   "Read"-ability 77
 16   Kinetics 83
 17   The "it's a small world" Effect 89
 18   Hidden Mickeys 95
 19   Plussing 101

PART THREE:
Imagineering Beyond the Berm 107

   20   Imagineering Game Design 109
   21   Imagineering Instructional Design 135
   22   Imagineering Management and Leadership 147

Post-Show: Final Thoughts and a Challenge 173
Appendix A: My Imagineering LIbrary 177
Appendix B: The Imagineering Pyramid Checklist 185

Bibliography 203
Acknowledgments 207
About the Imagineering Toolbox Series 209
About the Author 211
More Books from Theme Park Press 213

Foreword

How do they do that?

If you are like me, you have asked yourself that question a thousand times while experiencing the magic of Disney. Regardless of whether it is a moment of animation, a memory from an attraction, or the unmistakable ambiance of a theme park, our curiosity (one of Walt's most consistent character traits) inevitably gets the best of us. It is then that we just need to know, "How do they do that?"

Making magic isn't easy. But in the pages ahead, you have the opportunity to discover the method behind the magic. *The Imagineering Pyramid* provides the average layperson, people just like you and me, the opportunity to learn and apply the very principles the Imagineers use in creating and designing the most immersive attractions and theme parks in the world.

At some level, we all wish to bring home more than memories after visiting a Disney park. This is why Disneyland opened with souvenir shops on day one and we have been collecting Disneyana memorabilia ever since. The belief that your take-away can be more significant than a t-shirt, or even your own personalized pair of Mickey Ears, was my motivation for writing *The Wisdom of Walt: Leadership Lessons from The Happiest Place on Earth*. Disneyland is not just the place where dreams come true. Disneyland can be the place that inspires and shows us how to make our dreams come true.

Much to my delight, Lou Prosperi has taken this concept even further. Creativity is not an easy language to translate, but in the magical pages that follow you will see that Lou successfully shows us how to translate the work of the Imagineers into almost any creative endeavor. As a bonus, this course on creativity also allows us to discover some of the history behind the parks and hear stories about some of our most beloved attractions.

One of my favorite stories about the dream of Disneyland involves Walt's original work with architects who never could understand what it was that Walt wanted. Exasperated, the architects themselves eventually encouraged Walt to turn inward and find people on his own team who could build the stage and tell the stories that would one day become Disneyland. The architects who turned Walt down had in fact provided him with sage advice. Living in Southern California, I have the privilege of talking with folks who visited the park that first year, or maybe were even there on opening day. To a person they will say, "I had never seen anything like it. There was nothing like it anywhere in the world."

Walt's successful staff of studio craftsman would eventually evolve into the famed Imagineers who would go on to build not just Disneyland, but Disney parks and Disney attractions around the world, including the new Disneyland Shanghai, scheduled to open in 2016. Today, the Happiest Place on Earth is one of the most replicated places on earth. And to think it all started with a mouse—a mouse, a man, and a creative core of Imagineers who would push the limits of themed entertainment to heights never before believed possible or even imagined.

You can become your own replicator and be an "armchair Imagineer" by reading *The Imagineering Pyramid*. But don't just read this book; be sure to actually apply the pyramid's principles. Who knows, successful implementation could well result in someone experiencing your creative project and asking "How did you do that?"

Jeffrey A. Barnes, Ph.D.
California Baptist University

Preface: My Journey into Imagineering

"I bet that's him," my wife said as the young man walked past us.

"You think so? I guess we'll find out."

It was 11:20 on a Friday morning in late August, and we (my wife and kids and I) were waiting in the lobby of the Hollywood Brown Derby restaurant at Disney's Hollywood Studios theme park at Walt Disney World. We were there for the "Dining with an Imagineer" dining experience where you have lunch with one of the people who design and build Disney theme park attractions and shows.

As we waited in the lobby for our dining experience to begin, a young man (well, younger than me, anyway) wearing khaki shorts and a black polo jersey had just walked past us into the restaurant. Since the restaurant hadn't opened yet and the man hadn't checked in with the host, we figured he had to be a cast member (the Disney term for employee). We would soon discover that my wife was right, and that he was, in fact, "our" Imagineer.

For me, this lunch was the part of our trip that I was most looking forward to. The chance to talk with an Imagineer about Disney theme parks was something I just couldn't pass up. I had even tried to find out in advance the name of our Imagineer, in case it was someone I recognized, but the cast members at the restaurant either didn't know (which I think was the case) or didn't want to spoil the surprise.

Just after 11:30, the hostess led us, along with four other people, through the main dining room and into the Bamboo Room, a private area in the back of the restaurant where the young man in the khaki shorts and black jersey was waiting for us. The young man introduced himself as Jason Grandt, a senior concept designer, and we spent the next two-and-a-half hours enjoying a wonderful lunch and hearing stories about how the Imagineers work. He told us all sorts of stories, ranging from old ones about Walt Disney and some of the earliest

Imagineers, to more recent accounts of his own experiences. I felt like a kid on Christmas day.

So, why was this such a big deal to me? Well, to understand that, we need to go back in time…

My interest (some friends and family might say obsession) with Walt Disney World in general and Imagineering in specific began, not surprisingly, with my first visit to the park. It was in May 1993 when my wife and I went to Disney World on our honeymoon. Prior to this, my only exposure to the Disney theme parks was through pictures and TV, and while a picture may be worth a thousand words, that's still not enough to convey the true wonder, magic, and delight that I felt when I first experienced the "Most Magical Place on Earth" (not the "Happiest Place on Earth", which is the official tagline for Disneyland).

We started our visit at Epcot (or as it was known then, EPCOT Center). The park wasn't crowded at all, and we were able to walk onto nearly every attraction. We started with Spaceship Earth and made our way clockwise around Future World, starting in Future World East at the Universe of Energy, Wonders of Life, Horizons, and the World of Motion, followed by Future World West and Journey into Imagination, The Land, and The Living Seas.

While each of these attractions was more amazing than the last, exposing me to a type of entertainment I had never experienced or even imagined before, it was Journey into Imagination that really captured my imagination (pardon the pun) and began my journey along the path that would lead to that lunch with our Imagineer and writing this book. Following Dreamfinder and Figment along their "flight of fancy" that first time reminded me of the power of imagination and where it can take us. I had always been a kid at heart (or as a former girlfriend used to say, "childlike, not childish"), and that ride really spoke to the kid inside me.

You'll have to forgive the melodrama, but I believe that riding Journey into Imagination in May 1993 was a pivotal moment in my life.

And if Journey into Imagination had started my journey, my first visit to the Magic Kingdom the next day sealed the deal forever. There was no turning back. I remember being nearly awestruck seeing Cinderella Castle for the first time. It seemed like it couldn't be real, but there it was. I remember taking pictures of the castle from different angles, hoping to capture that feeling forever on film, but unfortunately, photography is not my strong suit. In the end it didn't matter. The magic born from Imagineering had implanted itself into my heart, mind, and soul, and I would never forget.

But just to help me keep the magic alive, I bought what books I could find about the parks, starting with a souvenir guide and a big full-color hardcover book entitled *Walt Disney World: Twenty Years of Magic*.

I found myself back at Disney World two years later, in 1995, along with my whole family, to celebrate my parents' 40th anniversary. I made sure to visit my friends Figment and Dreamfinder at Journey into Imagination a couple of times, and soaked in even more of the Imagineering magic. And of course, I bought more books. This time I found books about Walt Disney himself, including a book of his quotes and a biography (*The Man Behind the Magic: The Story of Walt Disney*), as well as a book about the Disney company (*The Disney Touch*, by Ron Grover). I had looked for more books about the parks and Imagineering, but back in those days, there simply weren't that many books about the subject to be had, or if there were, I couldn't find them. Years later I would learn about other Imagineering resources, such as *The "E" Ticket* magazine, but at that time, I was limited to what I could find at Disney World gift shops and in the local bookstore (and to what fit within my budget).

That changed in 1996 with the publication of *Walt Disney Imagineering: A Behind-the-Dreams Look at Making the Magic Real*. This was the first true glimpse I got into the process of how the Imagineers design and build Disney theme park attractions. It would turn out to be just the first of many items in my Imagineering library, but it would be awhile before I was able to add more.

Fast forward to 2005. Between 1996 and 2005, real life and other interests had (temporarily) drawn my attention away from Disney parks and Imagineering. During this time my wife and I had our first child (my son, Nathan), I returned to college to get my degree, we moved from Chicago back to Massachusetts, and then we had our second child (my daughter, Samantha).

My interest and passion in Disney parks was rekindled when we visited Walt Disney World again, this time with my wife's family to celebrate *her* parents' 40th anniversary. This was also the first time my kids had visited Disney World, and to see it through their eyes helped remind me of just how magical and special a place it can be. During this trip I also learned there were lots of other books that would eventually join my Imagineering library. The book I bought while there was *The Imagineering Way: Ideas to Ignite Your Creativity*, a collection of essays and stories written by Disney Imagineers (including Jason Grandt, the Imagineer we would meet a few years later) about creativity and the creative process. It was another look into the Imagineering process, and it re-ignited my interest in Imagineering. From that point on, I began tracking down every book or resource I could about Imagineering, Disney theme parks, and Disney in general.

Since that time, I've been to Disney World several more times, and have added dozens of books to my Imagineering library. Some of the highlights of my library include John Hench's *Designing Disney: Imagineering and the Art of the Show*; Karal Marling's *Designing Disney's Theme Parks: The Architecture of Reassurance*; Jeff Kurtti's *Walt Disney's Imagineering Legends and the Genesis of the Disney Theme Park*; Jason Surrell's books about the Haunted Mansion, Pirates of the Caribbean, and the Disney Mountains; the *Imagineering Field Guides* by Alex Wright; and many, many others.

As I added each new book to my Imagineering library, I didn't just read each and set it aside. I *studied* each one, often cross-checking stories and references across other books in my library to make sure I understood how it all fit together. I've read some of the books in my library four or five times (in particular, Alex Wright's *Imagineering Field Guide* series, which I've also indexed). Each time I re-read a book I come away with some new distinction or discovery. I even transcribed the entire Imagineering glossary from *Walt Disney Imagineering: A Behind the Dreams Look at Making More Magic Real* , word for word. (I told you my family might say I'm obsessed.)

As if I wasn't already obsessed enough, my interest in Imagineering got an additional boost when I had an "a-ha" moment that would further deepen my interest in Imagineering and eventually lead to our lunch with an Imagineer and to this book. How is that? Well, one day I was reading *Pirates of the Caribbean: From the Magic Kingdom to the Movies* by Jason Surrell (not for the first time) and I came across the following:

> In a ride system, you only have a few seconds to say something about a figure through your art, Blaine [Gibson] told Randy Bright. So we exaggerate their features, especially the facial features, so they can be quickly and easily understood from a distance.

I was working as a technical writer and trainer at the time, and as I read those words, I thought to myself "that's like what we do when we develop training materials—we simplify concepts and ideas so that students can understand them quickly and easily" (something I now call "read"-ability).

As I began to look at Imagineering through the lens of instructional design, I realized that many of the techniques and principles used by Walt Disney Imagineering could also have applications not just for instructional design, but across a wide variety of activities that lie outside the parks, or "beyond the berm".

If I had been eager to find new books about Imagineering before, this grew my appetite even more. I scoured every book in my library (and continued to add new ones), looking for the principles behind the practices, the hows and whys that explain how Imagineering magic really works. And as you might guess, I found further examples of how the Imagineering processes and practices could be applied to instructional design and other creative fields.

It was this continued search that was a main driver for my wanting to have that lunch with an Imagineer (you didn't think I'd get back to that, did you?). I wanted to be able to pick the Imagineer's brain about their processes, techniques, and "theory". I tried my best to scale back my enthusiasm and not completely dominate the conversation, but I'm not sure how well I succeeded. The lunch exceeded my expectations. Our Imagineer was a gracious host, the food was excellent (especially the Double Vanilla Bean Crème Brûlée), and his answers to my questions helped me clarify some of the distinctions I had been making about how Imagineering works.

My ongoing journey into Imagineering is also what brought about this book. The concepts of the Imagineering Pyramid outlined herein first took form as a presentation about instructional design called "The Imagineering Model: Instructional Design in the Happiest Place on Earth" that I gave to some curriculum developer colleagues. I later expanded and refined the material and presented "The Imagineering Model: What Disney Theme Parks Can Teach Us About Instructional Design" at a Society for Applied Learning Technology (SALT) conference in Orlando in 2011 (during which I also visited Disney World. Big surprise, I know!) Then, in early 2014, I presented a third version (renamed as "The Imagineering Model: Applying Disney Theme Park Design Principles to Instructional Design") as a SALT webinar.

I posted both versions of the presentation on Scribd and SlideShare, and caught the attention of Theme Park Press, who reached out to me about expanding the presentation into a book.

I'm still buying Imagineering books, both old and new, and am still on my journey into Imagineering. This book is a next step in that journey, and I'm glad to have you along for this part of it.

Introduction

I've been fortunate to have been involved in a number of creative fields for much of my adult life. When I first went to college, I studied music composition, and in addition to my original music, I also wrote several arrangements for a small jazz ensemble. Later I worked for as a freelance game designer before getting a full-time position as a product line developer for a small game company. After leaving that job, I did more freelance game design work, then worked for nine years years as a technical writer and trainer. For the past six years, I've served as the manager of a team of technical writers and curriculum developers for a small business unit in a large enterprise software company.

Now, I know what some of you may be thinking: "Music and game design are creative fields, but technical writing and training? Those don't seem all that creative." I disagree. I believe that there is a creative aspect to nearly everything we do. Even the most seemingly mundane of activities involves some level of creativity.

I'm not alone in this belief in the diverse nature of creativity. In *The Creative Habit: Learn It and Use It for Life*, renowned choreographer Twyla Tharp writes: "Creativity is not just for artists. It's for business people looking for a new way to close a sale; it's for engineers trying to solve a problem; it's for parents who want their children to see the world in more than one way." In their book *Creative Confidence: Unleashing the Creative Potential Within Us All*, authors Tom Kelley and David Kelly refer to the idea that creativity is something that applies only to some people as 'the creativity myth'. It is a myth that far too many people share." They also tell us: "Creativity is much broader and more universal than what people typically consider the 'artistic' fields. We think of creativity as using your imagination to create something new in the world. Creativity comes into play wherever you have the opportunity to generate new ideas, solutions, or approaches."

Likewise, I believe everyone is creative, even the people who tell you that they "don't have a creative bone in their body". The challenge for many of us lies in finding the right model of how creativity and the creative process works so we can apply it in our own fields. This book is my attempt at providing just such a model. But before we get to that, let's look at that word "creativity" a bit.

Creativity is a "magnetic" word for me. It draws my attention like a magnet.

You know when you buy a new car, suddenly you see that car everywhere? You may have never noticed it before, but now, everywhere you look there's a car just like yours. Did all those people *also* just buy the same type of car? Most likely not. What's happened is that your brain and perceptions have become more sensitive to that type of car because it's important to you. This recently happened to my wife and I when we bought a new car. One or two days after buying that car, I started noticing it on the roads far more often than I ever had before.

A similar thing happens when we set goals. After we've set a goal and gotten specific about what we can do to accomplish that goal, we start noticing more things that can contribute to us accomplishing that goal. Our brain filters out input that doesn't help us make progress on our goals, freeing us up to notice all those things that can help.

I have a similar experience with certain words, and I suspect the same is true for many of us. I think most of us have our own magnetic words, related to whatever it is that interests us, and those words capture our attention more than others. Some of my magnetic words include "Disney", "Imagineering", "imagination", "creativity", and "innovation". When I stumble upon an online article, blog, or Facebook post about any one of these, it immediately captures my attention and I spend a few moments investigating. Most times I quickly scan the item to see if it's something I want to devote more time to, and if so, I either make a note of it or spend a few minutes reading further. I also intentionally seek out online content about some of these words as well. I have Google Alerts set up for "Disney", "Imagineering", and "creativity", among others, and get daily updates with links to various online sources related to each.

I said earlier that I suspect many of us have own set of magnetic words. Some of those may be unique, but many of us also share magnetic words with those who share common interests. For instance, I strongly suspect that I'm not alone in having "Disney" or "Imagineering" among my magnetic words. I would guess that many of you are reading this book because of your own interest in

Disney and Imagineering. And while some words are magnetic to only a (relatively) small number of people, some are shared by so many that they become nearly universal. Creativity is one of the latter. Over the last several years, creativity has gained more and more attention, and has become a buzz word in business. In a blog post called "Creativity Creep" from September 2, 2014, on *The New Yorker* website, Joshua Rothman writes:

> Every culture elects some central virtues, and creativity is one of ours. In fact, right now, we're living through a creativity boom. Few qualities are more sought after, few skills more envied. Everyone wants to be more creative—how else, we think, can we become fully realized people?
>
> Creativity is now a literary genre unto itself: every year, more and more creativity books promise to teach creativity to the uncreative. A tower of them has risen on my desk—Ed Catmull and Amy Wallace's *Creativity, Inc.*; Philip Petit's *Creativity: The Perfect Crime*—each aiming to "unleash", "unblock", or "start the flow" of creativity at home, in the arts, or at work. Work-based creativity, especially, is a growth area. In *Creativity on Demand*, one of the business-minded books, the creativity guru Michael Gelb reports on a 2010 survey conducted by IBM's Institute for Business Values, which asked fifteen hundred chief executives what they valued in their employees. "Although 'execution' and 'engagement' continue to be highly valued," Gelb reports, "the CEOs had a new number-one priority: creativity," which is now seen as "the key to successful leadership in an increasingly complex world."

And so, if creativity is in such high demand, where can we turn to help us cultivate and develop our own creativity? Many of us turn to books. As Rothman notes, creativity has almost become its own literary genre, with dozens of books being published every year covering different aspects of creativity. Beyond books, the internet offers a seemingly endless array of online articles and blog posts focused on creativity as well, and nearly every day there are new items posted.

But even with all of the books and online content, I still think there's something missing from the "creativity literature". My observation is that the creativity literature seems focused on two main areas: 1) theory about creativity (traits of creative people, etc.) and 2) tips and techniques to help us "be more creative" or "generate new ideas".

While these are both valuable and useful to people wanting to be more creative, from my point of view what's missing is a model for the creative process—an example that we can look to for concepts and principles that can be applied across a variety of creative fields (and remember, there is a creative aspect to nearly everything we do).

Now. you might be asking, "Isn't being more creative a good thing?" Well, I suppose, but what exactly does "being more creative" even mean? Isn't it important to come up with new ideas? Again, I suppose it is, but the challenge here is this: ideas are easy—it's execution that's difficult. The real work is in taking those ideas and making them real. Put another way, generating ideas—sometimes also known as brainstorming or ideation—is not all there is to creativity. It's important, to be sure, but it's only a part of the challenge of employing our creativity. What's equally (or perhaps more) important is how we follow through and develop and/or implement our creative ideas.

Related to this is another important aspect to creativity that is rarely found in the creativity literature, namely, promoting and communicating our creative ideas to others. If we don't find ways to share our ideas and effectively communicate and promote them, they often go unrecognized, or worse, unrealized.

In his book, *The Myths of Creativity*, David Burkus outlines ten myths about creativity and explores the truths behinds those myths. This book is an excellent example of what I consider creativity theory, and should be in the library of anyone interested in creativity or in how we can be more creative. One of the myths explored in this book is the "Mousetrap Myth", or the idea that "once you have a creative idea or innovative new product, getting others to see its value is the easy part, and that if you develop a great idea, the world will willingly embrace it." The chapter on the Mousetrap Myth (the final chapter in the book) explores the flaws with the thinking behind this myth. The first is that, quite often, new creative ideas are seen as a challenge and/or a threat to the status quo, and are therefore either ignored or shunned. One of the best examples is Kodak ignoring the potential of digital photography (which they invented) because it challenged their market dominance in film and film processing. Burkus also explores the flawed idea that people with creative ideas often think the idea will speak for itself, and so don't work at promoting and communicating their ideas. Failure to promote and communicate has led many creatives to watch their ideas either die in a drawer, or be developed and marketed by someone else. As Burkus notes, "We don't just need more great ideas; we need to spread the great ideas we already have."

I wrote earlier that I believe the challenge for many of us lies in finding the right model of how creativity and the creative process works so we can apply it in our own fields. I think there is an assumption that people can apply their own expertise or technical know-how to take their ideas to the next level. And while there may be some truth to that, examples and models of taking an idea and shepherding it through the process of turning it into a reality seem to be few and far between.

So where can we look for a model or example of the creative process, and developing and communicating our creative ideas? I think one of the best places to look is Disneyland and other Disney theme parks. More specifically, I believe *one of the best models for creativity is found in the design and development of Disney theme parks, a practice better known as Imagineering.*

As we'll examine in more detail in the first part of this book, Imagineering was born from the blending of expertise from a number of fields. Just as the first Imagineers adopted techniques and practices from animation and movie-making to develop the craft of Imagineering, we can borrow (and steal) principles and practices from Imagineering and apply them to other creative endeavors.

In the foreword to Jeff Barnes' *The Wisdom of Walt: Leadership Lessons from the Happiest Place on Earth*, Garner Holt and Bill Butler of Garner Holt Productions (the world's largest maker of audio-animatronics) write: "Disneyland is still the ultimate expression of the creative arts: it *is* film, it *is* theater, it *is* fine art, it *is* architecture, it *is* history, it *is* music. Disneyland offers to us professionally (and to everyone who seeks it) a primer in bold imagination in nearly every genre imaginable."

If you look at what goes into the design and construction of Disney theme parks and attractions, you discover that Imagineering combines several disciplines often associated with creativity (including illustration, art direction, writing, music and sound design, interior design, lighting design, and architecture) as well as disciplines not typically considered creative such as various engineering fields (structural, mechanical, electrical, and industrial), project management, research and development, and construction management.

As a source of inspiration about creativity and the creative process, Imagineering has few peers.

In my search to learn as much as I could about how the Imagineers design and build Disney theme parks and attractions, I've identified a set of principles that I believe can serve as a model for the creative process in a variety of fields. I call this set of concepts the *Imagineering Pyramid*, and it contains principles focused on developing and communicating our ideas. These principles can be applied to developing nearly any type of creative project, from a simple homework assignment to a fully immersive theme park attraction such as Expedition Everest at Disney's Animal Kingdom.

The rest of this book is divided into three primary parts:

Part One: Pre-Show—Peeking over the Berm presents the origins of "Imagineering" and what the word means, as well as an overview of the Imagineering Pyramid. This will give us a foundation on which we can expand in later chapters. We'll also look briefly at the idea of having a "vision" and how that fuels the creative process.

Part Two: The Imagineering Pyramid is the heart of the book, and examines fifteen techniques and practices used by Walt Disney Imagineering in the design and construction of Disney theme parks and attractions. Starting with a look at something called the art of the show, this section contains chapters devoted to each block in the Imagineering Pyramid. For each block, we'll look at examples from the Disney parks, the principles behind each, and how each can be leveraged in other fields.

Part Three: Imagineering Beyond the Berm explores how to apply the principles of the Imagineering Pyramid to a number of specific fields, including game design, instructional design, and leadership and management.

Following Part Three is a "post-show" chapter in which I share some final thoughts and a pair of appendices. Appendix A contains a list of the books, DVDs, and other resources in my Imagineering library (as of this printing, anyway—it doesn't stay the same for long). Appendix B contains a checklist of questions based on the principles of the Imagineering Pyramid that you can use when developing, evaluating, and promoting your creative ideas.

PART ONE
Pre-Show:
Peeking over the Berm

When you first approach a Disney theme park, it's common that you might see the upper portions of some attractions peeking out over the park's perimeter or berm. These exposed structures give guests a peek at what they'll experience once they enter the park. (As we'll discuss in a later chapter, these structures act like "wienies", but I'm getting ahead of myself.) In this section, we're going to take a quick peek at Imagineering and the concepts that make up the Imagineering Pyramid.

- Chapter 1 looks at the origins of Imagineering and explores what "Imagineering" really means
- Chapter 2 provides an overview of the Imagineering Pyramid itself
- Chapter 3 discusses vision and how it informs the creative process

The goal of this section is to introduce you to tools in the Imagineering Pyramid, and to provide some context for the more in-depth discussion of the Imagineering Pyramid principles that comprise the bulk of the book.

CHAPTER ONE
What is Imagineering?

There's really no secret about our approach. We keep moving forward—opening new doors and doing new things—because we're curious. And curiosity keeps leading us down new paths. We're always exploring and experimenting ... we call it "Imagineering"— the blending of creative imagination and technical know-how.

— Walt Disney

In this chapter, I want to lay the groundwork for the rest of the book by exploring what Imagineering means, where the practice of Imagineering came from, and why it's a subject worth studying. This will provide some context for the later chapters of this book, and will establish a solid footing for our discussion of Imagineering practices and techniques.

What's in a Word?

In technical terms, "Imagineering" is a portmanteau (the blending of two or more words into a new word) formed from "imagination" and "engineering". Contrary to Disney mythology, Walt Disney didn't create the word. "Imagineering" was used by Alcoa in the 1940s in their advertising and marketing to promote what they considered to be imaginative approaches to engineering. But while he may not have coined the term, Walt Disney certainly popularized it when he used it on his *Disneyland* TV show to promote the Disneyland theme park.

Based on its origins, we could think of Imagineering simply as "the combination of imagination and engineering", but that definition falls a little flat for me, particularly when it comes to Disney theme parks. I think it's the word "engineering" that doesn't work for me.

While engineering certainly plays a part in Disney theme parks and attractions, the word has technical and scientific connotations not generally associated with other creative or artistic fields that also play significant a part in the design of Disney theme parks and resorts.

A better definition comes from the opening quote of this chapter. Walt Disney defined Imagineering as *the blending of creative imagination and technical know-how*. I like this definition for two reasons. First, it adds the word "creative" to highlight the importance of creativity in imagination. Second, "technical know-how" is a broader term than engineering and encompasses technical and scientific expertise as well as creative and artistic expertise, and is a better reflection of the varied range of disciplines practiced by Disney Imagineers.

The general nature of Walt's definition also means that it applies to a wider range of people and activities. Based on this definition, anyone who has ever used their imagination in the context of some sort of technical know-how has engaged in Imagineering, whether they know it or not.

Think about it. The "blending of creative imagination and technical know-how" isn't restricted to theme park design, or even to other so-called creative fields. It can apply to any sort of task, even those that most of us might consider mundane. A file clerk who devises a new filing system can be thought to have "imagineered" the new system. A chef who combines spices and sauces in unique ways might be thought of as a "cooking or culinary imagineer". A science teacher who incorporates games and other activities into the classroom to help students learn is "imagineering" their lesson plan. In short, everyone, including you, has practiced Imagineering in one form or another at some point in their lives.

But the fact that we've all practiced Imagineering isn't what makes it a good model and example for developing and promoting creative ideas. There's more to it than that.

To understand why Imagineering is such an effective model for creative projects in other fields, we first have to look more closely at how Disney's Imagineers employ their creative imagination and apply their technical know-how when designing and building theme parks and attractions. In other words, we need to look more specifically at how Disney Imagineers practice Imagineering. We'll explore many aspects of this in later sections, but we need to start with a look at its origins and roots.

Imagineering Origins

Walt Disney Imagineering (WDI) is the division of The Walt Disney Company responsible for the design and development of Disney theme parks, resorts, cruise ships, shopping areas, and other venues and attractions. Walt Disney Imagineering is the modern incarnation of WED Enterprises (named after Walt's initials, **W**alter **E**lias **D**isney), the organization originally formed by Walt Disney that was charged with the design and construction of Disneyland. It was WED that gave birth to Imagineering.

So, how did this organization come to be?

To answer that question, and to understand how Imagineering came to be the art form and craft that it is today, we need to go back in time and look at the origins of WED Enterprises and Disneyland.

When Walt Disney first began planning for Disneyland, he approached his friend and noted Los Angeles architect Welton Becket about working on the project. In what has become a famous story in Disney and Imagineering history, Becket told Walt that he should use his own people, because they understood the type of storytelling he was looking for with Disneyland. In his foreword to Jeff Kurtti's *Walt Disney's Imagineering Legends and the Genesis of the Disney Theme Park*, Marty Sklar retells this story:

> It [Disneyland] might never have happened if Walt Disney's friend and neighbor, Los Angeles architect Welton Becket, had coveted the design job. For when Walt approached him about designing Disneyland, and explained the concept brewing in his head, Mr. Becket gave his friend this advice: "You'll use architects and engineers, of course, but Walt—you'll really have to train your own people; they are the only ones who will understand how to accomplish your idea.

In 1952, Walt Disney formed WED Enterprises as a company to manage his personal interests and projects, among them the design of Disneyland. Following the advice he got from Becket, the first people Walt brought into WED were artists and art directors from his own studio who worked on early designs for Disneyland. Over time he added others, including model makers, architects, story men, and machinists. As the plans for Disneyland expanded, even more disciplines found their way into WED, such as sculptors, show writers, special effects engineers, songwriters, landscape architects, and lighting designers. When WED took on additional projects, such as designing attractions for the 1964–1965 New York World's Fair and early planning for what would become Walt Disney World, it grew to include even more diverse types of artisans, craftsmen, and engineers.

Each of these early Imagineers brought with them experience and expertise in other fields that they adapted to the design of Disneyland and other Imagineering projects. Film and animation techniques such as forced perspective, cross-dissolves, and sight gags, once confined to two-dimensional stories told in film and animation, found new expressions in the three-dimensional storytelling that was evolving at Disneyland. Over time, other techniques and practices such as theming and the use of wienies were tried, tested, and perfected, adding even more tools to the Imagineering repertoire. Over the years, the various disciplines within WED continued to expand to include electrical engineers, sound design engineers, electronic engineers, ride system engineers, and show control engineers. Today the Imagineers at Walt Disney Imagineering span more than 140 disciplines.

Based on practices and principles borrowed and adopted from these varied disciplines, over time WED developed its own methodologies, techniques, and processes for designing and building attractions. Taken together these have become what we know today as the art and craft of Imagineering. As described by blogger "Merlin Jones" on the *Re-Imagineering* blog on May 18, 2006:

> Out of WED's Imagineering braintrust came the theories, aesthetics, design and engineering of Disneyland, the advancement of three-dimensional storytelling, the development of robotic techniques in audio-animatronics and the perpetuation of an "architecture of reassurance" as inspired by Walt Disney's personal sense of optimistic futurism.

In later chapters of his book, Jeff Kurtti recounts the story of Welton Becket's advice no less than three more times, including one of his chapter introductions and quotes in at least two of the essays about the original Imagineers. Kurtti's recounting of this story emphasizes its importance to the birth of WED and to the craft of Imagineering. For our purposes, the importance of the story is that it shines a light on how we can learn from Imagineering.

Imagineering is a craft based on adapting skills, knowledge, and expertise from one medium and applying them to another. Imagineer Alex Wright describes the parallels between developing animated films and theme park attractions in this excerpt from *The Imagineering Field Guide to Disneyland*:

> The act of designing a "dark ride" ... is very similar to that of developing an animated short film. Many of the same techniques are brought to bear, and we go through many of the same steps in the process. We outline our story. We storyboard it. We spend time coming up with gags to make it fun. We integrate the design with any dialog needed to advance the action. We fine-tune (fine-toon) our timing and pacing, and assess the payoff of the story. Even today, the Imagineers rely on the model set out for us by the animators of the Walt Disney Studios, especially those who made the transition from animation to Imagineering and created this new art form.

Imagineering was born from the combined experience and expertise of these early Imagineers, who brought with them technical know-how from film, animation, and other fields and adapted that know-how to the new form of entertainment of which Disneyland was the first example—the theme park. And just as the first Imagineers adopted techniques and principles from film-making when they developed the craft of Imagineering for the design of Disneyland, *we can adopt the techniques and principles of Imagineering in other fields, such as game design and instructional design.*

That's really what this book is all about. It's a close look at the principles behind the techniques used in Imagineering—the tools the Imagineers use in the design and construction of Disney theme parks—with an eye toward applying those same principles to other fields—fields that lay "beyond the berm".

CHAPTER TWO
A Quick Look at the Pyramid

The Imagineering Pyramid is a arrangement of fifteen important Imagineering principles, techniques, and practices used by Walt Disney Imagineering in the design and construction of Disney theme parks and attractions. We'll look at each of the blocks of the pyramid in more detail in Part Two, but for this chapter let's start with a high-level look at the pyramid and the principles.

The principles in the Imagineering Pyramid each fall into one of five categories or groupings, each of which forms a tier within the pyramid.

The Tiers of the Imagineering Pyramid

- Walt's Cardinal Rule
- Making It Memorable
- Visual Communication
- Wayfinding
- Foundations of Imagineering

Tier 1: Foundations of Imagineering

The bottom tier of the pyramid includes the foundations, or "cornerstones", of Imagineering. These principles serve as the base upon which all other techniques and practices are built. There are five Imagineering foundations:

- **It All Begins with a Story** Using your subject matter to inform all decisions about your project
- **Creative Intent** Staying focused on your objective
- **Attention to Detail** Paying attention to every detail
- **Theming** Using appropriate details to strengthen your story and support your creative intent
- **Long, Medium, and Close Shots** Organizing your message to lead your audience from the general to the specific

Tier 2: Wayfinding

The second tier is focused on navigation and guiding and leading the audience, including how to grab their attention, how to lead them from one area to another, and how to lead them into and out of an attraction. The four Wayfinding principles include:

- **Wienies** Attracting your audience's attention and capturing their interest
- **Transitions** Making changes as smooth and seamless as possible
- **Storyboards** Focusing on the big picture
- **Pre-Shows and Post-Shows** Introducing and reinforcing your story to help your audience get and stay engaged

Tier 3: Visual Communication

The third tier includes techniques of visual communication that are used throughout the parks in different ways. You'll find examples of these in nearly every land and attraction. These principles include:

- **Forced Perspective** Using the illusion of size to help communicate your message
- **"Read"-ability** Simplifying complex subjects
- **Kinetics** Keeping the experience dynamic and active

Tier 4: Making it Memorable

The fourth tier includes practices focused on reinforcing ideas and engaging the audience. It is the use of these techniques which helps make visits to Disney parks memorable. These include:

- **The "it's a small world" Effect** Using repetition and reinforcement to make your audience's experience and your message memorable
- **Hidden Mickeys** Involving and engaging your audience

Tier 5: Walt's Cardinal Rule

The top tier contains a single fundamental practice employed in all the other principles. I call it "Walt Disney's Cardinal Rule":

- **Plussing** Consistently asking, "How do I make this better?"

The following diagram illustrates how these principles are arranged within the Imagineering Pyramid:

The Imagineering Pyramid

- Plussing
- The "it's a small world" Effect
- Hidden Mickeys
- Forced Perspective
- "Read"-ability
- Kinetics
- Wienies
- Transitions
- Storyboards
- Pre-Shows and Post-Shows
- It All Begins with a Story
- Creative Intent
- Attention to Detail
- Theming
- Long, Medium, and Close Shots

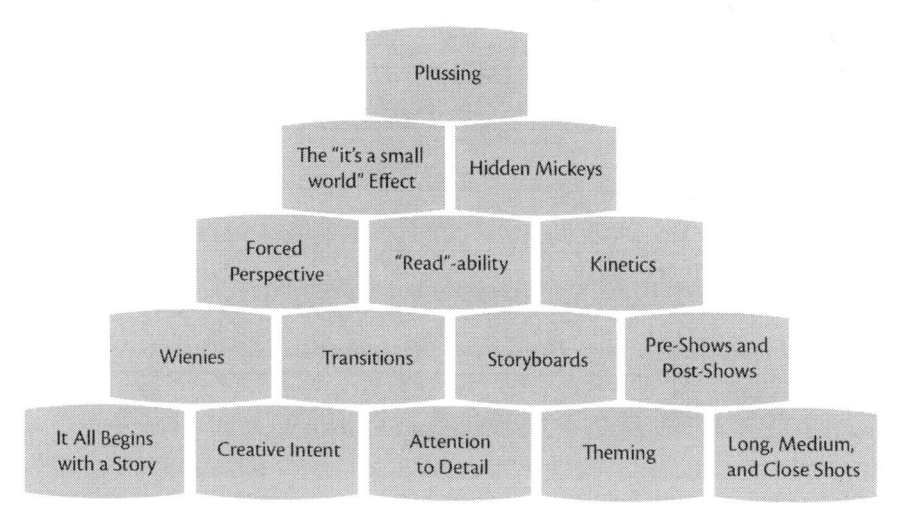

CHAPTER THREE
Imagineering and the Power of Vision

Before we dive into the individual principles and practices of the Imagineering Pyramid, I want to first look at a fundamental element of every creative endeavor, and the role it plays in the creative process. Whether you're creating an entire theme park, a single attraction, or something as simple as a short presentation, *the core of every creative project is a vision*—a picture of what the project will look like when it's complete. A creative vision can be as grandiose as Walt Disney's vision for EPCOT (the Experimental Prototype Community Of Tomorrow) or much more modest and simple. In either case, a vision is at the heart of the creative process.

One of my favorite depictions of the power of vision is an image entitled, appropriately enough, "VISION" that depicts a parcel of undeveloped land in Orlando, Florida, where Walt Disney World would eventually be built, with images of Walt Disney and Cinderella Castle superimposed over the land. The caption for this image is one of Walt Disney's more famous quotes: "It's kind of fun to do the impossible." For me, this one simple image sums up the idea of vision perfectly.

Vision was central to nearly everything Walt Disney created, including his animated masterpieces such as *Snow White and Seven Dwarfs*, his live-action films such as *Mary Poppins*, and what some consider his most significant achievement, Disneyland. Walt had a compelling vision for each project he worked on, and was able to share that vision with the animators, filmmakers, and Imagineers who helped bring his ideas to reality. It was that shared vision that enabled Walt to draw out the best from all the people who worked with him. There have been few creators like Walt Disney who had the ability to develop and share their vision so effectively. I think it's fair to say that Walt's vision and his ability to infectiously share that vision with those around him are the true source of the "Disney magic" that so many fans of his work admire and enjoy.

Walt's vision for what would eventually become Walt Disney World outlived him, and has become a significant part of his ongoing legacy. In *How To Be Like Walt: Capturing the Disney Magic Every Day of Your Life*, Pat Williams and Jim Denney share an oft-told story about Walt's vision for Disney World:

> Though Walt envisioned Walt Disney World in Florida, he died before it was built. On opening day in 1971, almost five years after his death, someone commented to Mike Vance, creative director of Walt Disney Studios, "Isn't it too bad Walt Disney didn't live to see this?"
>
> "He did see it," Vance replied simply. "That's why it's here."

I've seen many, many different versions of this story, featuring various people in the "He did see it..." role. The one consistent element in all of the iterations is the idea that "Walt saw it, that's why you're seeing it". It was his vision that was the inspiration and basis of what Walt Disney World would become.

The same can be true of you and your projects. A compelling vision fuels the creative process, and can serve as both inspiration and motivation as you work your way through the steps of bringing your vision to life.

Just as Walt Disney's visions for *Snow White*, *Mary Poppins*, Disneyland, and Disney World inspired his animators, filmmakers, and Imagineers, a clear vision can help inspire you when you develop your creative projects. If you're working with others on your projects, it's important that you share your vision with them and get them excited about it as well. And, as we'll see in later chapters, the principles of the Imagineering Pyramid can help not only in developing your creative ideas, but also when communicating and promoting them to others.

PART TWO
The Imagineering Pyramid

In Part Two, we're going to look at each of the blocks of the Imagineering Pyramid in more detail. The chapters in this section explore the techniques, practices, and principles in the Imagineers' toolbox, including how they are employed in the Disney parks, as well as how each can be applied "beyond the berm" in other fields and creative projects. We're also going to look at how everything the Imagineers do comes together in the "art of the show".

In addition, each of the chapters in this part include a section entitled Post-Show: Imagineering Checklist that summarizes the main ideas of the chapter and offers questions to get you thinking about how you can apply the ideas in that chapter to your own creative projects.

The Imagineering Pyramid

- Plussing
- The "it's a small world" Effect | Hidden Mickeys
- Forced Perspective | "Read"-ability | Kinetics
- Wienies | Transitions | Storyboards | Pre-Shows and Post-Shows
- It All Begins with a Story | Creative Intent | Attention to Detail | Theming | Long, Medium, and Close Shots

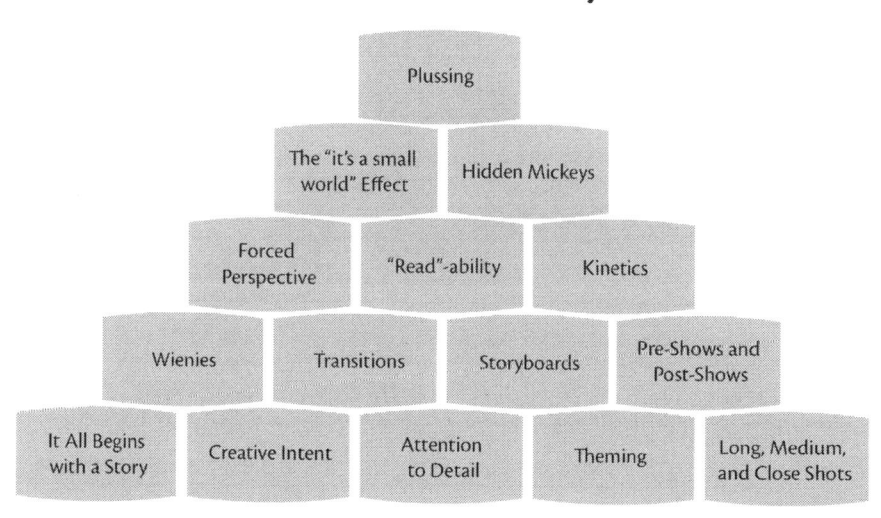

CHAPTER FOUR
The Art of the Show

The Imagineering Pyramid

(Pyramid diagram with blocks labeled: Plussing; The "It's a small world" Effect; Hidden Mickeys; Forced Perspective; Readability; Kinetics; Wienies; Transitions; Storyboards; Pre-Shows and Post-Shows; It All Begins with a Story; Creative Intent; Attention to Detail; Theming; Long, Medium, and Close Shots — overlaid with the text "The Art of the Show")

Before we explore the Imagineering Pyramid in detail, I want to first talk about how they all come together in "The Art of the Show".

In his book *Designing Disney: Imagineering and the Art of the Show*, Imagineer John Hench notes that "Walt realized that a visit to an amusement park could be like a theatrical experience—in a word, a sh*ow*. Walt saw that guests' sense of progressing through a narrative, living out a *story* told visually, could link together the great variety of attractions he envisioned for his new kind of park."

The concept of "show" is very important to Walt Disney Imagineering, and to the Disney company as a whole; it permeates the company's culture and behavior. Much of the language used within the Disney company has it roots in show business. The people who work for the company aren't employees or workers, they're cast members. The areas of the parks that guests are allowed to see are referred to as "onstage" areas, while areas considered off limits to guests are known as "backstage" (behind the scenes). Even the terms that Imagineers use to describe the quality and condition of the parks and attractions are "good show" and "bad show".

In the *Imagineering Field Guide* series, Imagineer Alex Wright elaborates on this, noting "[Show is] everything we put 'onstage' in a Disney park. Walt believed that everything we put out for the guests in our parks was part of a big show, so much of our terminology originated in the show business world. With that in mind, show becomes for us a very broad term that includes just about everything our guests see, hear, smell, or come in contact with during their visit to any of our parks or resorts."

So what is the art of the show? According to John Hench, "Designing the guest's experience is what Walt's Imagineers came to call 'the art of the show', a term that applies to what we do at every level, from the broadest conceptual outlines to the smallest details, encompassing visual storytelling, characters, and color."

Another definition comes from Hench's obituary on the MousePlanet website on February 10, 2004, written by Sheila Hagen, who writes: "Hench was a master of the 'art of the show', a philosophy that demanded that every design element contributed to the story or helped to create a natural visual segue from one themed land to another."

Because the Disney "show" includes everything guests see, hear, smell, or come in contact with when they visit Disney parks or resorts, practicing the art of the show means that every action the Imagineers take and every decision they make is based on whether or not that action or decision contributes to the "show". In everything they do, every decision they make, the Imagineers are clear on their objective. Their goal is to entertain their audience. All too often in creative projects contributors are overcome by details, project plans, and deadlines, and lose sight of their primary outcome. With a construction deadline looming and a tight budget, it's easy to forget that the entire reason for the project is to create an entertaining experience. By focusing on the art of the show, the Imagineers stay grounded to their original creative intent, and don't get overwhelmed by the minutiae of their day-to-day activities.

Knowing Your Mission

In simpler terms, practicing the art of the show is how the Imagineers stay focused on their overall objective: entertaining their audience, and putting on a "show" for the guests. In other words, practicing the art of the show means *knowing your mission, and ensuring that everything you do contributes to that mission.*

This means that you need to know what your mission is and what business you're really in. And while that may sound like a silly statement ("Of course we know what business we're in!"), the history of business includes many examples of industries and businesses that lost sight of their mission and the business they were actually in, and suffered as a result. Theodore Levitt explores this idea in an article called *Marketing Myopia* in the July 2004 issue of *Harvard Business Review*:

> Every major industry was once a growth industry. But some that are now riding a wave of growth enthusiasm are very much in the shadow of decline. Others that are thought of as seasoned growth industries have actually stopped growing. In every case, the reason growth is threatened, slowed, or stopped is not because the market is saturated. It is because there has been a failure of management.
>
> ... The failure is at the top. The executives responsible for it, in the last analysis, are those who deal with broad aims and policies. Thus:
>
> - The railroads did not stop growing because the need for passenger and freight transportation declined. That grew. The railroads are in trouble today not because that need was filled by others (cars, trucks, airplanes, and even telephones) but because it was not filled by the railroads themselves. They let others take customers away from them because they assumed themselves to be in the railroad business rather than in the transportation business. The reason they defined their industry incorrectly was that they were railroad oriented instead of transportation oriented; they were product oriented instead of customer oriented.
>
> - Hollywood barely escaped being totally ravished by television. Actually, all the established film companies went through drastic reorganizations. Some simply disappeared. All of them got into trouble not because of TV's inroads but because of their own myopia. As with the railroads, Hollywood defined its business incorrectly. It thought it was in the movie business when it was actually in the entertainment business. "Movies" implied a specific, limited product. This produced a fatuous contentment that from the beginning

led producers to view TV as a threat. Hollywood scorned and rejected TV when it should have welcomed it as an opportunity—an opportunity to expand the entertainment business.

... There are other, less obvious examples of industries that have been and are now endangering their futures by improperly defining their purposes.

These examples illustrate that it's not uncommon for businesses to get so focused on what they do (trains and movies) that they lose sight of their real purpose (transportation and entertainment). And while these examples represent entire industries, the same principle applies to individual businesses, business units operating within larger organizations, and even your own personal creative projects.

Understanding the distinction between your mission or purpose and the activities you perform as part of that mission is important. Your mission isn't what you do, it's why you do it. For example, in my current job I manage a team of technical writers for a small business unit within a large enterprise software company. One of the things we do is produce various types of product documentation such as user guides and installation guides. But that's not our mission. Our end mission is to help our customers get the most value out of our products. Producing documentation is simply the means to that end. In the railroad and Hollywood examples, the industries in question found themselves at risk because they confused the way in which they did things with their true purpose and mission. They failed to take advantage of new opportunities because they lost sight of their mission—they didn't practice the art of the show.

Post-Show: Imagineering Checklist

The Art of the Show is *knowing your mission, and ensuring that everything you do contributes to that mission.* Your mission isn't what you do, it's why you do it.

- What is your "show"? What business are you really in? What is your mission?
- Look at the various activities you perform on a day to day basis. Do they all contribute to your "show"?
- Do you have a metaphor that communicates your mission like "show" does for Walt Disney Imagineering?

CHAPTER FIVE
It All Begins with a Story

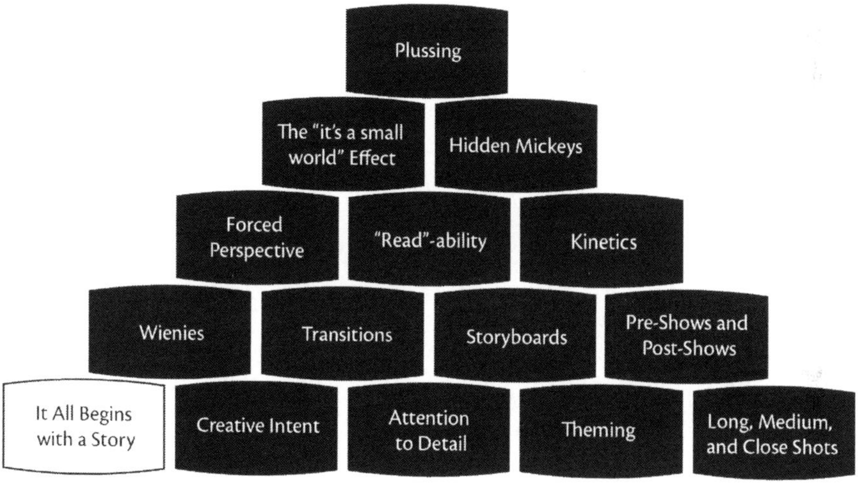
Plussing
The "it's a small world" Effect
Hidden Mickeys
Forced Perspective
"Read"-ability
Kinetics
Wienies
Transitions
Storyboards
Pre-Shows and Post-Shows
It All Begins with a Story
Creative Intent
Attention to Detail
Theming
Long, Medium, and Close Shots

> *Story is the essential organizing principle behind the design of the Disney theme parks.... When we design any area of a Disney theme park, we transform a space into a story place. Every element must work together to create an identity that supports the story of that place....*

This quote, taken from Imagineer John Hench's *Designing Disney*, underscores the significance of story in the design of Disney theme parks, and is the first block in the Imagineering Pyramid. This block is the first of the foundations of Imagineering, and is one of the cornerstones of Imagineering. Simply put, it all begins with a story...

Story is the fundamental building block of everything Walt Disney Imagineering (WDI) does when designing and building attractions. The Imagineers identify a core idea for each attraction they build, and it is that core idea, or story, that serves as the basis for every detail of the attraction. Decisions about an attraction's theming (another tool that we will discuss later), lighting, sound effects, background music (BGM in Imagineering parlance), and other details are all based on how well they serve to support the story.

Examples of this are everywhere in Disney's theme parks. Fantasyland dark rides such as Peter Pan's Flight, Snow White's Scary Adventures, and Pinocchio's Daring Adventure at Disneyland each contain scenes taken straight from the classic animated films upon which they are based. Other examples can be found in Cinderella Castle in Magic Kingdom at Walt Disney World. In the castle breezeway, a series of mosaics depict scenes from the story of Cinderella, and the columns between these mosaics are topped with sculptures of Jac and Gus, the mice who Cinderella befriends in the story. The scenes in Pirates of the Caribbean help evoke the story of pirates attacking and looting a Caribbean port city, while scenes in the Haunted Mansion evoke the "aura of foreboding" that permeates that attraction.

The specific ways in which story is expressed in Disney attractions span a wide range including graphic design, nomenclature, color, and character paint and plaster. Every detail of every attraction designed by the Imagineers is informed by its story.

That said, the importance of story to the Imagineers doesn't mean that every attraction tells a story; instead, it suggests that every attraction is based upon a story. Also, an attraction's story is not always (or even often) a fleshed-out narrative (as in having plot, characters, with a beginning, middle, and end, etc.). Sometimes the story behind an attraction is better described as a theme or concept than what we often think of when we think of the word story. For example, "it's a small world" doesn't have a story in the traditional sense, but it does have a strong core idea. Likewise, the original versions of the Haunted Mansion and Pirates of the Caribbean at Disneyland don't tell a specific story. What these three attractions have in common is that each is built upon a strong concept that informs their every detail.

An attraction's story is usually born during the "blue sky" stage that marks the beginning of the Imagineering process, and is later shaped, molded, and formalized during later phases of the project. During these later phases, the story serves its role as the core idea that the Imagineers refer to when faced with design challenges.

Story vs Storytelling

Imagineering has been using story as its "essential organizing principle" since their earliest days during the design of Disneyland, but the idea that "Imagineers are storytellers" is a more recent one, born during Michael Eisner's tenure as CEO and chairman of The Walt Disney Company. Eisner frequently commented on the importance of stories and storytelling in the Disney theme parks, to the point where the meaning of the word story and its role in Imagineering has become somewhat clouded.

Overuse of the term story and the strong emphasis on story and storytelling employed by WDI is considered somewhat controversial on some internet blogs and discussion boards. Many online commentators believe that to say that Disney attractions all tell a story is to overly simplify what WDI does. Some critics even go as far as to suggest that the Imagineers at times rely too heavily on telling stories with their attractions. And while the idea that "Imagineers are storytellers" is often promoted by the Disney company in their own blogs and videos about WDI, there is an argument to be made that some of the original Imagineers didn't consider themselves storytellers at all.

One example is Disney animator an Imagineer Marc Davis, who didn't believe that theme park attractions were a storytelling medium. Davis went on record several times regarding his views.

In *The Unauthorized Story of Walt Disney's Haunted Mansion*, Jeff Baham quotes from "Marc Davis and the Art of the Haunted Mansion", an article publshed in issues 30–31 of *Haunted Attraction Magazine*:

> You know, the first guys that worked on [the Haunted Mansion] could never sell it to Walt because they were trying to sell this story about this bride who was left standing at the altar, and this groom had died a horrible death. The thing was, I found out—and Walt agreed—that this was not a story-telling medium. These attractions at Disneyland and Disney World are experiences, but they are not stories. You don't have a story that starts at a beginning and goes until the end.... These things I worked on had no story at all, and I think they worked, too.

In *The Disneyland Story*, Sam Gennawey quotes Davis from issue number 16 of *The "E-Ticket"* magazine:

> My point of view on all of these attractions is that they are a series of experiences. You aren't telling a story in the Haunted Mansion any more than you are trying to tell a story in Pirates of the Caribbean.

> You're showing some pirates in a lot of interesting situations, but you don't really have a beginning or an ending. They're a series of situations, not a story. I think that is why Walt never bought the Haunted Mansion in his time.

Davis believed that theme park attractions provide their audiences not with a story, but with a series of experiences. In his resignation letter, Imagineer Tony Baxter writes: "Legendary Imagineer Marc Davis once said, 'We don't really have a story with a beginning, an end or a plot.... It's more a series of experiences ... building up to a climax.'"

In a letter to Jack and Leon Janzen from *The "E-Ticket"* magazine, Imagineer Christopher Merritt quotes Marc Davis when he writes:

> I think it [the Hatbox Ghost] was a good idea at the time. Remember, the mansion had been worked on for a number of years, and Walt had never bought what they had come up with. I don't recall why we took this [the Hatbox Ghost] out, but we were no longer trying to tell a story about the bride. Walt's attitude was that he didn't want a story, but a series of experiences and situations. Perhaps this figure didn't lend itself to this.

In an essay that opens the Imagineering chapter of the book *Marc Davis: Walt Disney's Renaissance Man*, Imagineering executive Marty Sklar acknowledges Davis' views, saying: "In joining the Imagineers to create what he called "experience rides", Marc Davis became the most prolific Imagineer of his time in developing ideas and drawings for Disney park attractions."

But even if we agree with Davis, that doesn't mean that story hasn't been, and isn't still, a foundational tool in the Imagineers' toolbox. I believe some detractors have gotten themselves too hung up on the word "story" and some of its narrative connotations, and this has led them to forget the role that story has always played in the design of Disney theme parks. As Didier Ghez writes in *Disneyland Paris: From Sketch to Reality*:

> Walt Disney was, foremost, a storyteller.
>
> As a result, everything starts with a story at Walt Disney Imagineering. Every detail of every land in the park has to be backed up by a story, a "mythology". Often, the story would never be a part of what the guests would experience, but was used as a strategic outline in guiding the design process. It is the thread that holds it all together, the script from which all the elements flow coherently: design, models, color, backdrops, props and costumes.

And it's the essence that distinguishes a Disney park and its lands from all other parks.

"Story", then, serves as an elegant shorthand for "the core idea that underlies each attraction". I recently discovered that this view is shared by at least one current Imagineer. In an essay entitled "A Story by Any Other Name" in *The Imagineering Field Guide to Disney California Adventure at Disneyland Resort*, Imagineer Alex Wright explores the idea of story and explains how WDI employs a broad definition of story that is intended to encompass all manner of experiences that guests encounter in Disney parks. In his words:

> It's often said that everything we do at Imagineering is about story—and it is. But that phrase in and of itself is really just shorthand for a much more nuanced idea of what "story" means in our medium of Disney parks. It doesn't mean the same thing that it would mean if we were writing a book, making a movie, drawing a comic strip, or even standing on a stage telling a story to an audience. None of those media are approached in exactly the same way by the creators in those fields, so why would we expect that this one wouldn't follow its own path?

Following this introductory paragraph, Wright examines how story can have different meanings depending on the type of attraction or venue, and how guests serve as collaborators in the storytelling that takes place in the parks.

Story Equals Subject Matter

In the world outside the parks—beyond the berm—what Imagineers call story is your subject matter. What is your project all about? What is the core message of your project? The Imagineers' story serves as the basis for every detail of an attraction, and your subject matter should be the foundation of every aspect of your project. Put another way, "it all begins with a story" means *using your subject matter to inform all decisions about your project.*

Just as the Imagineers base their decisions about their attractions on their core idea or story, you should base decisions about your project on its core idea. When focusing on details, the details you choose to employ should always relate to and help support your story. If you're working on a marketing presentation about a specific product, that product is your story and every piece of information you choose to include should in some way help promote your product.

When making decisions about your project, your subject matter should serve as a guideline in terms of what does and does not belong. For instance, in the world of instructional design and training development (which we'll look at in more detail in Part Three), your story is the subject matter of your training. If you're creating training about first aid, you wouldn't want to devote time to a treatise on blood types. While it might be considered a related topic, training about first aid is not the best place for that type of information, and including it could distract the audience from the real topic at hand.

The Pyramid in Practice— It All Begins with a Story

As we move through the Imagineering Pyramid, I'm going to spend a few words discussing how I've tried to apply each principle to this book. Note that word "tried".

My story in this book is Imagineering, focusing on the principles and practices employed by the Imagineers in the Disney theme parks and how those same principles and practices can be employed in other fields. As we explore the design principles in the Imagineering Pyramid, there is a lot more I could say about many of these, but I'm trying to focus each chapter on specific examples both within and beyond the berm that help illustrate each principle, and not include long tangential discussions about some of the more esoteric aspects of themed entertainment. For example, in this chapter I debated including a discussion about the nature of the "Disney show" and the role of "reassurance" in the success of the Disney parks, but that discussion really doesn't fit with my story and so in the end I opted to leave that out.

Post-Show: Imagineering Checklist

It All Begins with a Story is *using your subject matter to inform all decisions about your project*. Story is the essential organizing principle behind the design of the Disney theme parks.

- What is your "story"?
- What is your subject matter? What is your project about?
- Are you basing decisions about your project on your subject matter?

CHAPTER SIX
Creative Intent

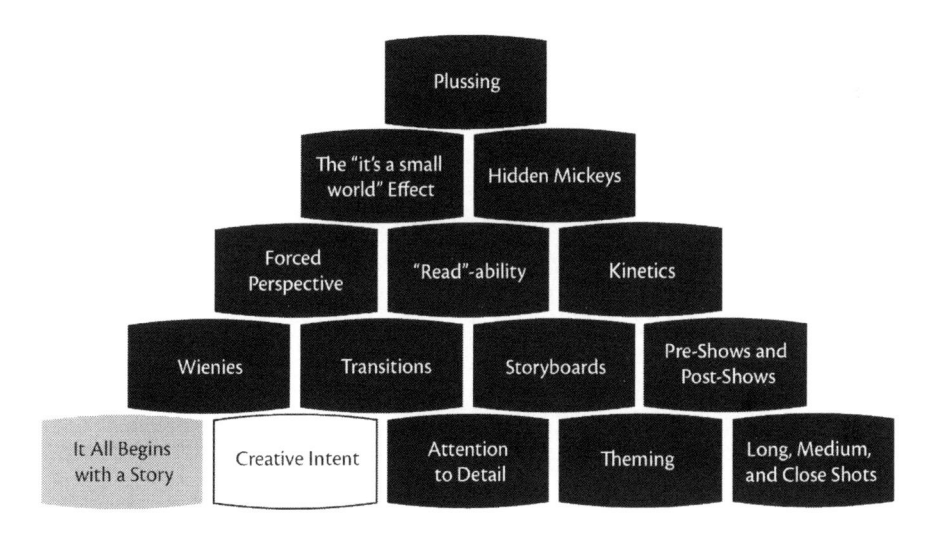

The next block in the Imagineering Pyramid, and the second of our foundations of Imagineering, has to do with identifying and understanding the specific creative objectives of each particular attraction or venue within the "show". This specific creative objective is what's known in Imagineering lingo as *creative intent*.

In *Walt Disney Imagineering: A Behind the Dreams Look at Making MORE Magic Real*, creative intent is defined as "what the designers want to accomplish; they are the guardians and arbiters of the creative intent of the built environment".

Creative intent can be thought of as the specific design goals the designers want to accomplish with a specific project. Put another way, *a project's creative intent defines the experience the designer hopes to create for their audience.*

The creative intent of an attraction is nearly always related directly to the attraction's story or theme (we looked at the role of story in the last chapter), and also typically addresses the need that spawned the project in the first place. For example, if the original need that led to the development of Expedition Everest at Disney's Animal Kingdom were something as simple as "Animal Kingdom needs a thrill ride", the creative intent might be described as "have guests experience a runaway train ride in the Himalayas that culminates in to a face-to-face encounter with the Yeti!" This not only relates directly to the story of that attraction, but also addresses the original need.

Creative intent is often defined during the initial blue-sky stage in the Imagineering process, but isn't something that Imagineers focus on only at the beginning of a project. It remains a focus throughout the life of the attraction, even after the attraction has opened. A goal of WDI's Show Quality Standards group is to ensure that the original creative intent of an attraction isn't diluted or changed over time (unless of course it is intentionally changed as part of a renovation).

Let's look at some examples of the creative intent of some attractions in the parks at Walt Disney World. The short descriptions that appear in park guide maps and websites often convey (or at least hint at) each attraction's creative intent:

- **Big Thunder Mountain Railroad** Streak through a haunted gold-mining town aboard a rollicking runaway mine train.
- **Buzz Lightyear's Space Ranger Spin** Fire lasers to defeat Zurg in this shooting-gallery game that puts you in the center of a thrilling space battle.
- **Expedition Everest—Legend of the Forbidden Mountain** Careen through the Himalayan mountains on a speeding train while avoiding the clutches of the mythic Abominable Snowman.
- **Haunted Mansion** A spine-tingling tour through an eerie haunted estate, home to ghosts, ghouls, and supernatural surprises.
- **"it's a small world"** Embark on a whimsical boat ride past a jubilant confection of singing children from around the globe.
- **Kilimanjaro Safaris** Ride off in an open-air vehicle for a tour of a lush African savanna, home to exotic animals like lions and elephants.

- **Pirates of the Caribbean** Set sail on a swashbuckling voyage to a long-forgotten time and place when pirates and privateers ruled the seas.
- **Seven Dwarfs Mine Train** Race through the diamond mine from *Snow White and the Seven Dwarfs* on an adventurous family coaster.
- **Soarin'** Take flight and feel the wind through your hair as you fly above breath-taking vistas of California.
- **Star Tours** Feel the power of the Force during a 3D, motion-simulated space flight that launches you into the world of *Star Wars*.
- **Space Mountain** Blast off on a rip-roaring rocket through the darkest reaches of outer space.
- **Test Track** Create your own virtual concept vehicle and put it through the paces on the exhilarating hills, hairpin turns and straightaways of the Test Track circuit.
- **The Twilight Zone Tower of Terror** Take a thrilling elevator ride in the Twilight Zone aboard a haunted elevator.

Notice how all but one of these starts with a verb, helping to set the stage for the experience that park guests will enjoy. Each description explains, vividly, what guests will experience on the attraction.

In addition to the information in guide maps, the creative intent of an attraction can be conveyed in its "pre-show" through specific theming and details, which often provide enough information for guests to have an idea of what they'll experience.

For example, when moving through the queue and pre-show at Expedition Everest, guests learn that "Himalayan Escapes—Tours and Expeditions" offers train service to the base of Mount Everest crossing over the Forbidden Mountain. As guests make their way through the Yeti Museum, they see artifacts, legends, and "facts" about the Yeti, the mysterious creature believed to live on the Forbidden Mountain, as well as remnants of past expeditions there. These details set the stage for what guests will experience aboard their train.

Another great example of conveying creative intent through theming and details can be found at the Bibbidi Bobbidi Boutique, located in the breezeway of Cinderella Castle at Walt Disney World. The Bibbidi Bobbidi Boutique is a salon where young female guests can get a princess makeover, including the hairstyle, makeup, and costume of their favorite Disney princess. As guests walk through the breezeway from the central plaza or "hub" toward Fantasyland, the boutique is on the left amid the mosaics that depict the story of Cinderella.

My family and I met the designer of the Bibbidi Bobbidi Boutique—(then) Senior Concept Designer Jason Grandt—when we visited Walt Disney World a number of years ago at our "lunch with an Imagineer". One of the stories Jason shared was about creative intent, specifically his creative intent for designing the Bibbidi Bobbidi Boutique. His first goal was to create an environment that men find uncomfortable. He said this mostly tongue-in-cheek, but I got the impression that the overall aesthetic he was aiming for was one that didn't generally appeal to men, so I think there may be some truth to it. The second, and more serious goal (and more to our point here), was to create an environment where the young girls having their makeovers should think that Cinderella herself might show up at any moment.

So, how did the Imagineers go about creating an environment where the young girls having princess makeovers would think that Cinderella might show up at any moment? Let's look at the venue itself. Just inside the entrance of the boutique is a sign that reads as follows:

Image Copyright © Michelle Davis

Hear ye, Hear ye!
All loyal subjects of the
Magic Kingdom
are hereby notified
by royal proclamation
of a ball to be held
this very day
in your honor.
the
Royal Princess
Cinderella
and our noble
Prince Charming
humbly request
the pleasure of your company
at this magical event.

Your humble servant,
the Grand Duke

This is a proclamation that there will be a ball tonight, and all are invited. Young guests of the Bibbidi Bobbidi Boutique aren't simply getting a princess makeover. They're preparing for the Grand Duke's ball, the very same ball that Cinderella and Prince Charming will be attending. That means that as the young guests are being readied for the ball, at any moment Cinderella herself may show up to get herself ready. The story of the venue—the story of the Grand Duke's ball—embodies its creative intent. This is a simple and fairly straightforward example, but I think its simplicity helps illustrate the idea better than a more involved or less obvious example might.

Staying Focused on Your Objective

In the world "beyond the berm", focusing on creative intent means *staying focused on your objective*. We want to make sure that everything we do when developing and promoting our creative projects serves the underlying objective of the project.

Of course, the only way you can stay focused on your objective is to be clear on what that objective is. Like companies and industries and people can lose sight of their mission (as we discussed in Chapter 4), it's not uncommon for people and companies to lose sight of the true objective of an activity by getting caught up in the details of performing it. For example, if you decide to take up running as a way to get in better shape and lose weight, running isn't your objective. Improving your physical condition and losing weight are your objectives. Running is the means to that objective.

As another example, the business unit I work for sells enterprise software to the utility industry to help with billing, data management, network and grid operations, and other business processes. A long-held belief of our business is that companies are looking for software that can be customized or tailored to the utility's specific business processes. That's changing. Instead of insisting that the software change to meet their business processes, some utilities are willing to change their business processes to accommodate the software they select. One of the reasons is that these companies are realizing that their existing business processes aren't their real objectives. Those processes were developed at one time to help meet a specific objective, but now these same objectives can also be met in other (often more efficient and less costly) ways. By focusing on their true objectives, these companies become more open to the idea of changing the way they do business.

Vision and Creative Intent

Your project's creative intent will almost always be strongly based on your vision for the project. Of all of the principles in the Imagineering Pyramid, creative intent is the one most closely related to vision, as it gets to the heart of what you want to accomplish with your project.

One key idea when defining your creative intent is that your objective should be more than to simply create something. The thing you create is simply a vehicle to get your audience to experience something. Your goal isn't simply to create an example or artifact of your discipline. When designing attractions for Disney parks, the Imagineers' goal isn't just to create another attraction. It's to add a specific experience to the overall show. Whatever field you're working in, whether it be theme park design, game design, graphic design, or instructional design, your goal shouldn't be to create an artifact, be it a ride, or game, or illustration, or training course. It's to create an experience for your audience, whether that audience be an actual audience at a performance or event, a participant in an activity such as a game, a customer or client, or a student in a training class.

As I mentioned earlier, creative intent isn't something the Imagineers focus on only during the design and construction of an attraction. The Imagineers remain focused on creative intent after the attraction has opened and they continue to focus on it for the life of the attraction. Likewise, if your creative projects have an extended lifespan, it's important to occasionally evaluate whether or not they're still fulfilling the objective you had when you first created the project. For example, if you develop a system or process in your work to help solve a problem or a challenge, once it's been solved you may find that it's time to retire that process or system. Sometimes we continue to do things long after they've served their purpose because those activities become "the way we've always done things". Staying focused on your objective can help prevent you from falling into routines that no longer serve your needs. We'll look at this idea again in Chapter 22 (Imagineering Management and Leadership).

By the way, if you notice a similarity between creative intent and the art of the show, that's by design. In some ways, creative intent can be thought of as the smaller-scale cousin to the art of the show. The show is the larger-scale mission, while the creative intent is the specific objective of each part of the show. In an earlier version of the pyramid, the art of the show was one of the foundation blocks and creative intent was discussed as part of that block. I later decided that each of these principles, while related, were different enough to warrant separate discussion.

Focusing on your creative intent—your objective—can also help act as a filter when determining which ideas or concepts to include in your project. What has happened to me on more than one occasion is that when brainstorming ideas for a project I'll get a great idea—well, what I think is a great idea—but unfortunately, when filtered through the lens of my original objective, I realize that my "great" idea really doesn't fit as well as I thought it would. This is not unlike how your story can help determine which details to include in your project.

The Pyramid in Practice—Creative Intent

My creative intent with this book is fairly obvious—to explore the principles and practices of Imagineering with a particular focus on how they can be applied to other fields. To this end, I've included a variety of examples throughout, as well as separate chapters focused on applying the Imagineering Pyramid to a handful of specific fields, including game design, instructional design, and leadership and management.

Post-Show: Imagineering Checklist

Creative Intent is *staying focused on your objective*. A project's creative intent defines the experience the designer hopes to create for their audience.

- What is your objective? What is your creative intent?
- What is the experience you want your audience to have?
- As you evaluate decisions and next steps in the life of your project, ask yourself, "Does this help me move closer to achieving my objective?"

CHAPTER SEVEN
Attention to Detail

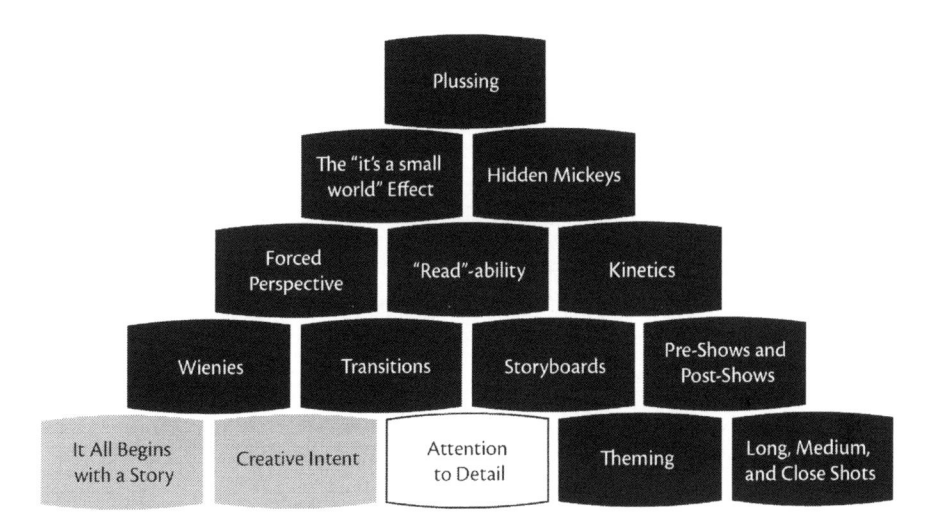

```
                    ┌─────────────┐
                    │   Plussing  │
                    └─────────────┘
            ┌──────────────┐  ┌──────────────┐
            │ The "it's a  │  │Hidden Mickeys│
            │ small world" │  │              │
            │   Effect     │  │              │
            └──────────────┘  └──────────────┘
      ┌──────────┐  ┌────────────┐  ┌──────────┐
      │  Forced  │  │"Read"-     │  │ Kinetics │
      │Perspective│ │ability     │  │          │
      └──────────┘  └────────────┘  └──────────┘
  ┌────────┐  ┌───────────┐  ┌──────────┐  ┌──────────────┐
  │Wienies │  │Transitions│  │Storyboards│ │Pre-Shows and │
  │        │  │           │  │          │  │ Post-Shows   │
  └────────┘  └───────────┘  └──────────┘  └──────────────┘
┌─────────┐ ┌─────────┐ ┌─────────┐ ┌────────┐ ┌──────────────┐
│It All   │ │Creative │ │Attention│ │Theming │ │Long, Medium, │
│Begins   │ │ Intent  │ │to Detail│ │        │ │and Close Shots│
│with a   │ │         │ │         │ │        │ │              │
│Story    │ │         │ │         │ │        │ │              │
└─────────┘ └─────────┘ └─────────┘ └────────┘ └──────────────┘
```

The next block of the Imagineering Pyramid is a key practice that Disney parks are known for—attention to detail. To help explain the importance and pervasiveness of attention to detail, let's start with the words of Imagineer John Hench, from *Designing Disney*:

> The minute details that produce the visual experience are really the true art of the Disney-themed show, its greatest source of strength. The details corroborate every story point, immersing guests into the story idea ... if one detail contradicts another, guests will feel let down or even deceived. This is why he [Walt] insisted that even details that some designers thought no guest would notice—such as the replicated period doorknobs on Main Street, U.S.A.—were important. Inappropriate details confuse a story's meaning.

If we think of the first two principles we've discussed (It All Begins with a Story and Creative Intent) as cornerstones of an Imagineering project, then Attention to Detail might be thought of as the mortar that holds the project together. Like the previous two principles, this one is basic and fundamental, and several other principles that we'll look at later are directly related to it.

Details of all kinds surround guests at Disney parks and resorts. Some are obvious, while others are more elusive, yet they all work together to create the environment and atmosphere of a Disney park that is so compelling and inviting. The types of details employed in the design and construction of a Disney park attraction are varied, yet all play a part in the overall experience.

There isn't enough room in this book to provide an exhaustive look at the details in the Disney parks (several books on the subject have been published if you're interested), but let's look at a handful of examples of attention to detail from the Disney parks and resorts.

Liberty Square in Magic Kingdom at Walt Disney World is a great place to start.

- In the Hall of Presidents, all of the clothing worn by the audio-animatronics figures are authentic reproductions of the respective eras in which the presidents lived. For instance, the clothes on the Abraham Lincoln figure are authentic reproductions of the post-Civil War era. This focus on details extends even to details the audience can't see, including the braces on the Franklin Delano Roosevelt figure's legs.
- The street numbers on the buildings in Liberty Square indicate the year from which the building's architecture is derived.
- Liberty Square is one of the few lands in the Magic Kingdom without public restrooms, because they did not exist in Colonial times.

Another great source of examples of attention to detail is in the use of color. According to Alex Wright, John Hench was "largely responsible for refining [the Imagineers'] philosophies of color" and personally worked on defining the colors used on several attractions.

- There are seven shades of gray for the stone trim at different elevations on Cinderella Castle.
- The exterior of The American Adventure pavilion at Epcot uses four different shades of white in the trim from the bottom of the building to the top. Reasons for this variety of shades of white include accounting for the ambient light in Florida, the color

of the Florida sky, and the way in which the different shades of white interact with the building's other colors.

- In his foreword to John Hench's *Designing Disney*, Marty Sklar shares a story about the construction of The Living Seas Pavilion at Epcot. According to the story, an executive from the sponsor company told Hench that he wanted the pavilion painted "bright white". Hench's reply was, "Sir, there are thirty-three shades of white in my palette—do you have a favorite?"

But while attention to detail is important, an equally important distinction is recognizing that there are appropriate places for details. It can be a fine balancing act between too much and too little detail, and over the years the Imagineers have become experts at riding that line to near perfection. Let's look again at what John Hench tells us about details, in *Designing Disney*:

> A detail should only be used if it is essential to the story in some way. There is a big difference between being overwhelmed with detail that really amounts to clutter, and the feeling of perfection that is real storytelling. As designers, we must not make the mistake of thinking that a "big look" with lots of detail is enough.

As noted above, other principles in our Imagineering Pyramid are related to attention to detail, and serve as examples of some specific ways in which the Imagineers employ details in the design of Disney parks and attractions. A couple of specific examples include the last two foundations of Imagineering (Theming and Long, Medium, and Close Shots) which focus on the types of details to employ and how those details are used and arranged to help support the show and the story. We'll look at these in the following two chapters.

Paying Attention to Every Detail

The principle underlying this tool is straightforward enough. This is all about *paying attention to every detail*. Accurate and appropriate details support your story and help communicate your ideas and your creative intent. Incorrect or inconsistent details can interfere with the communication of your message.

When considering the details of your creative projects, you should focus on details that apply to your subject matter and contribute to your creative intent. Here is where we see that the tools in the

Imagineering Pyramid don't all stand alone. These concepts relate to one another, and the decisions you make in regard to one tool may impact how you employ other tools.

One of the plain and simple truths about discussing details is that *details draw attention to themselves*. Consider word problems in middle school and high school math class. Often one of the keys to solving those problems is to identify which details to focus on, and which to ignore. The more detail you employ, the closer your audience is likely to look at your project, so any details you employ need to be correct. A further consequence is that we must take care when deciding when, where, and how to employ details. For example:

- Introducing a detail too soon can cause your audience to focus on it more than necessary.
- Introducing a detail in an inappropriate place can distract your audience.
- Employing too much detail can overwhelm your audience (see the John Hench quote, above).
- Employing too little detail can confuse your audience

I experienced the first two of these when reading *The Art of Explanation: Making Your Ideas, Products, and Services Easier to Understand* by Lee Lefever. Chapter 13: "Bringing an Explanation Together" begins with the following sentences: "Meet Emma, a human resources manager of a large clothing retailer. Her company is in the middle of a big change: they're transitioning every employee to a new benefits system with a high deductible health plan. Emma is heading up the team that's been charged with communicating this change to employees." When I first read this, the phrase "high deductible health plan" jumped out at me and grabbed my attention. As I read on I kept waiting for more information about a "high deductible health plan", but the next two paragraphs made no mention of it. They were about Emma's plan to communicate a change to the employees in her company. The subject matter and objective of the chapter were about creating an explanation, but the inclusion of the "high deductible health plan" detail attracted my attention and distracted me from the chapter's real objective (if only for a few moments).

Another factor to keep in mind when looking at your use of detail in your projects is identifying the appropriate level of detail to employ; knowing how much is too much. There is a balance between not enough and too much detail; between being overwhelmed with details that really amount to clutter, and the feeling of carefully selected details. When trying to find the balance between too little and too much detail, a good place to start is by looking at your story and creative intent to make sure that the details you use support your subject matter and objective.

The Pyramid in Practice— Attention to Detail

I'm fairly detail oriented, and strive to make sure I get my details right in my writing. Some of the details I focused on when writing this book include the names of the blocks of the Imagineering Pyramid (some of which have changed over time), my sources, and the use of formatting and styles (using italics for names of films or books, for instance).

Post-Show: Imagineering Checklist

Attention to Detail is *paying attention to every detail*. Details draw attention to themselves.

- Are you paying attention to the details of your project?
- Does this detail support your subject matter or story?
- Does this detail support your creative intent?
- Are you including too much detail? Too little?

CHAPTER EIGHT
Theming

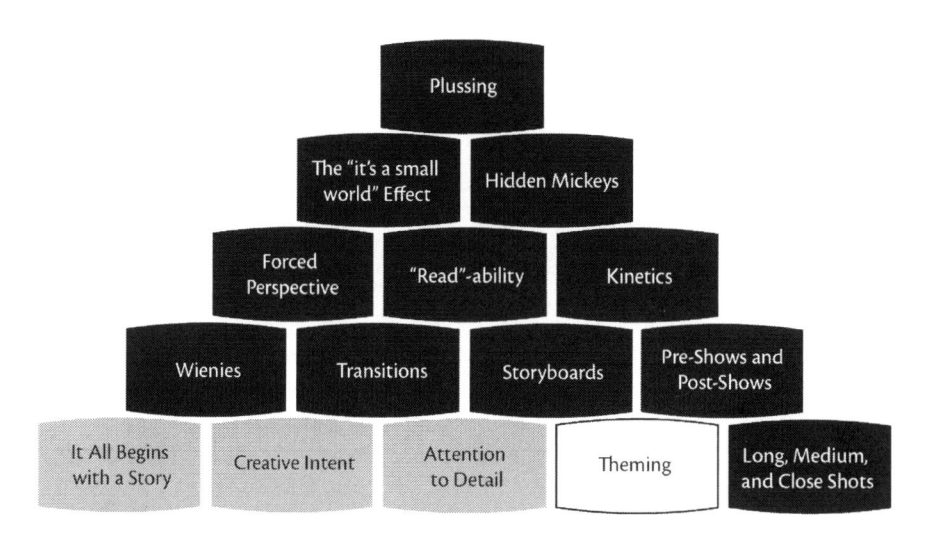

```
                    Plussing
        The "it's a small
          world" Effect        Hidden Mickeys
    Forced
  Perspective      "Read"-ability      Kinetics
                                              Pre-Shows and
  Wienies      Transitions    Storyboards      Post-Shows
It All Begins                  Attention                Long, Medium,
 with a Story  Creative Intent  to Detail   Theming    and Close Shots
```

In earlier chapters we've seen the importance of story and details in the design of Disney theme parks. In this chapter we're going to look at how these come together in the fourth block in the Foundation tier of the Imagineering Pyramid. This next principle can be thought of as the combination of It all Begins with a Story and Attention to Detail, and is called Theming.

Theming is all about selecting the right details to support your story or theme, and ensuring that everything in an attraction, resort, or park fits its story or theme. John Hench, in *Designing Disney*, tells us that "[t]he 'theming' of an attraction identifies it with a Disney story, and allows guests to experience that story through their senses". Theme is one of the most important things to come out of the blue sky and early stages of the Imagineering process. It is the fundamental nature of what a story is in terms of what it means to the Imagineers, and is really what sets Disney parks apart from amusement parks. An article entitled "Disney's Space Mountain" in issue 30 of *The "E" Ticket* magazine describes it this way:

> As he planned his first Magic Kingdom, Disneyland, Walt Disney is known to have purposely excluded many features and ride elements found in the conventional amusement parks of the past. Walt and his team used the resources of the Studio and their motion picture experience to create the theme park ... an unprecedented place where environments and entertainments blended magically to surround and enchant the visitor.

Theming is often employed at different "levels" within the Disney parks, including park-level, land-level, and attraction-level. For example, several lands within a particular park might share some aspects of theming, but often there are distinct differences in theming between different lands. For example, the theming employed in Adventureland in Magic Kingdom is different than the theming of Tomorrowland. Much of the theming in Adventureland takes the form of natural materials in the form of wooden hand rails and wooden/thatched walls, while the theming in Tomorrowland tends toward fabricated materials such as metal hand rails and brushed steel walls.

At the attraction level, each attraction within a single land might use its own unique theming elements. For example, both Maharajah Jungle Trek and Expedition Everest are located in Animal Kingdom's Asia and share some common theming elements, but they each also have their own distinct theming that sets them apart. The theming of Maharajah Jungle Trek is based on the jungles of southeast Asia while Expedition Everest's theming conjures its setting in the Himalayan mountains of Nepal.

In the Disney parks, theming is supported by many different types of details including the use of set decorating, props, and costumes. Set decorating is one of the more prominent of these, and has direct ties to Disney's roots in filmmaking. In *The Imagineering Guide to Disney's Hollywood Studios at Walt Disney World*, Imagineer Alex Wright writes:

> One of the disciplines of Imagineering most directly derived from the art of filmmaking is that of set decorating. In fact, we have a great many set decorators at WDI who have worked in the film industry. The intent of the role is the same in both media—to communicate to an audience with visual literacy and with an efficiency of design

the nature of a space and the people or characters who inhabit it. Set decorators make selections based upon the choices a character would make in creating the environment around them.

One of the ways the Imagineers ensure consistent theming within a park, land, or attraction is to define sets of rules that guide their decisions when adding details to their themed environments. These rules outline the types of colors, textures, and materials used in a particular environment (such as the examples from Adventureland and Tomorrowland, above) and other details.

Another tool used to ensure consistent theming in some lands and attractions is an architectural technique known as "kit-of-parts design". Examples can be found in A Bug's Land in Disney California Adventure, an area directly inspired by the Pixar film *A Bug's Life*. Wright continues:

> In kit-of-parts design, a defined set of elements—which can be configured in multiple ways to achieve the intent—is available to the designer. The logic of a kit-of-parts is applicable to the world of the bugs in the film and in our land because the "kit" is defined by the elements that would be available to the characters in order to build the world in which they live. In the case of *A Bug's Life*, the environment is comprised only of things that are within the reach of the bugs, either found in their natural environment or left behind by humans.

Yet another tool in the Imagineers' theming toolkit is known as an "eye wash", which involves the use of "graphics and set work that add atmosphere to an area but do not draw too much attention; for instance, the labeling on crates on Tom Sawyer Island," according to *Walt Disney Imagineering: A Behind-the-Dreams Look at Making MORE Magic Real*.

Another practice related to theming is that of "placemaking". In *The Imagineering Field Guide to Epcot at Walt Disney World*, Alex Wright explains that placemaking "is a prime function of WDI's designs, and a big reason our shows are successful. Place making involves crafting a setting of time and place that will provide the appropriate backdrop to our shows." When done effectively, lands and attractions feel "natural" and immerse guests into the experience such that the specific thematic details fade into the background and go largely unnoticed.

Theming is not limited to Disney's parks. Disney resorts (as well as cruise ships and other venues) are also great places to find examples of theming. For instance, tropical palms, koi ponds, and white sand beaches at the Polynesian Village Resort at Walt Disney World evoke an atmosphere reminiscent of the South Pacific while the nature trails, murmuring creeks, and totem poles of Wilderness Lodge (also at Disney World) create an environment inspired by the Great Northwest and turn-of-the-century national park lodges.

But theming isn't only used at the larger and more expensive resorts. Even less grandiose resorts make use of theming, albeit in different ways. A good example is the All-Star Movies Resort at Disney World. As the name implies, the resort is themed around movies. There are five pairs of buildings, each themed to a particular Disney film (*Toy Story*, *101 Dalmatians*, *Fantasia*, *The Mighty Ducks*, and *The Love Bug*). The design of the resort makes use of a movie filmstrip motif which can be found throughout, for example, the hand railings on the upper floors of the buildings, the design of the tiles in the bathroom showers, and even the backs of the chairs in the food court.

The filmstrip motif serves as a constant and subtle means of reinforcing the movie theme around which the resort is built. This is the sort of thing that would be easy to gloss over during the design of the resort, but its inclusion adds to the atmosphere in a subtle and not obvious way. I expect many guests don't consciously notice this use of detail, but it helps to tie everything in the resort together. Guests are surrounded by details that reinforce the idea that they are in a place that is "about movies".

Using Appropriate Details to Strengthen Your Story

Theming is all about *using appropriate details to strengthen your story and support your creative intent*. Theming means striving to make sure that your project delivers its message in a clear and consistent manner, one that supports and, if possible, enhances the intended experience. Inconsistent theming can distract and confuse your audience.

While many of the concepts in the Imagineering Pyramid take different forms inside and outside Disney theme parks, theming is one that is practiced in much the same manner both in Disney parks and in the world beyond the berm. Examples of theming in the outside world include themed restaurants such as the ESPN Zone, Planet Hollywood, and the Rainforest Cafe, as well as themed resorts and casinos in Las Vegas, including Luxor Las Vegas, Excalibur, and New York-New York.

Other examples of theming include branding and the use of corporate logos and slogans, or what we might call "corporate theming". Many companies have specific style guidelines for the use of colors, trade dress, and slogans to ensure that their communications and messaging employ consistent theming to support their corporate identity. Even small companies make use of theming in this way. One company I worked for used a very specific shade of blue (LODESTAR Blue) in all of its marketing and promotional materials.

One of my favorite examples of corporate theming is the company Life is Good, Inc. Wikipedia describes this company as follows: "Life is Good, Inc. is a New England–based apparel and accessories wholesaler, retailer, and lifestyle brand founded in 1994 and best known for its optimistic T-shirts and hats, many of which feature a smiling stick figure named Jake and the registered trademark 'Life is good'." Up until a recent branding change in 2015, the apparel created and sold by Life is Good, Inc. was very distinctive and employed consistent use of design, lettering, and illustration style. Their theming helped reinforce the company's mission of "Spreading the power of optimism" and their slogan "Do what you love. Love what you do."

A specific way in which many companies employ theming is corporate presentations. Consistent use of language and terminology, styles, and fonts and colors in presentations can help support communication by not distracting your audience. As noted earlier, inconsistent theming can distract your audience and take them out of the experience. This can be not just word choice or image choice, but inconsistent use of templates and formatting. For example, a few years ago I participated in a training class, and for the most part the slides used a consistent pair of fonts for headings and body text. However, one of the slides had four different fonts on it, and it really jarred me out of the subject matter, and drew my attention away from the topic at hand.

When done well, theming is hardly noticeable, yet subtly and quietly supports both your story and creative intent. At the same time, bad or inconsistent theming can lose your audience before you even have a chance to tell them your story.

The Pyramid in Practice—Theming

Many aspects of theming in this book (fonts, styles, etc.) are not in my hands, but in the hands of the book's designer. While I've made some suggestions, I trust my publisher to make the right choices here. Where I have made my best attempt at theming is in the consistent use of terminology and names for the ideas in this book. Several of the blocks of the Imagineering Pyramid have changed names over time, and I caught myself occasionally using older names while writing different sections and chapters of this book.

Post-Show: Imagineering Checklist

Theming is *using appropriate details to strengthen your story and support your creative intent*. Theming is the combination of It All Begins with a Story and Attention to Detail.

- Are you using details that support your story, and don't distract your audience?
- Are you being consistent in your use of language and terminology?
- Are you being consistent in your use of templates and formatting?

CHAPTER NINE
Long, Medium, and Close Shots

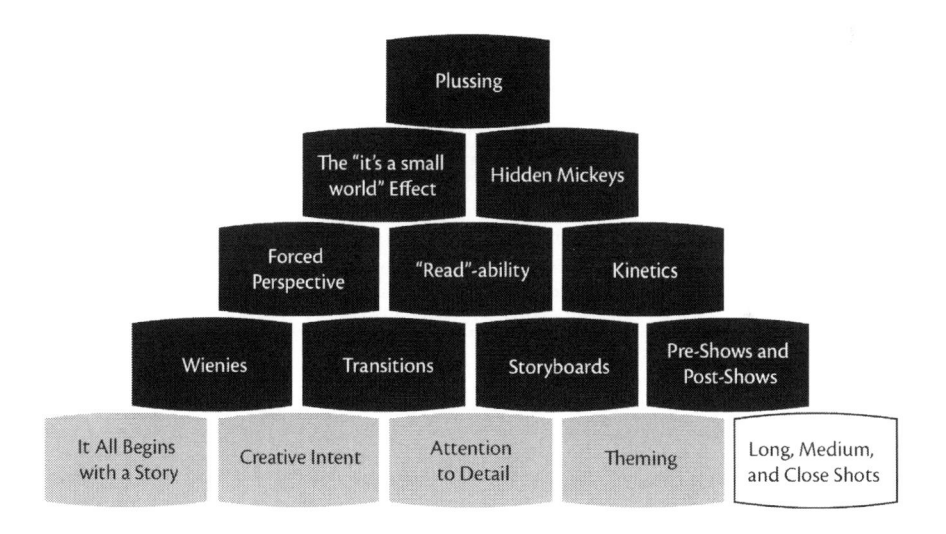

Pyramid diagram (bottom to top):
- Bottom row: It All Begins with a Story | Creative Intent | Attention to Detail | Theming | **Long, Medium, and Close Shots**
- Next row: Wienies | Transitions | Storyboards | Pre-Shows and Post-Shows
- Next row: Forced Perspective | "Read"-ability | Kinetics
- Next row: The "it's a small world" Effect | Hidden Mickeys
- Top: Plussing

As you walk down Main Street U.S.A. toward the central plaza in the Magic Kingdom, you see a large castle, adorned with spires, turrets, a drawbridge, and even a moat. As you draw closer, additional details come into view. You see the outlines of the individual stones used in creating the castle walls, the stained glass windows, gold leaf, and other details. This isn't simply a castle. It's a fairy-tale castle. As you move even closer, walking up along the ramps into the castle's breezeway, even greater levels of detail appear. Along the breezeway, a series of vast mosaics tell the story of Cinderella. The tops of the columns between the mosaics are carved with figurines of the mice who help Cinderella prepare for the ball. The details tell the story of Cinderella, and reinforce the idea that this is Cinderella Castle. This move from an establishing shot (a castle), through a medium shot that focuses on the idea (a fairy-tale castle), to details that tell the rest of the story (Cinderella Castle) is an example of the next block in the Imagineering Pyramid and the fifth and last of the foundations of Imagineering: Long, Medium, and Close Shots.

Like Theming, this tool is also closely related to Attention to Detail; if Theming is about using appropriate details to support your story, Long, Medium, and Close Shots is about arranging and organizing those details to help lead your audience into your experience. This practice borrows directly from the cinematic technique of using an establishing shot, and then moving in for a close up. One way to look at this practice is through the metaphor of a narrowing camera lens. With an establishing shot the lens captures the entire picture, but as you zoom in closer, the focus shifts to specific details that support the initial view.

In his *Imagineering Field Guide* series, Alex Wright explores how this practice is used by the Imagineers in the design of Disney parks:

- In *The Imagineering Field Guide to Disneyland*, Wright tells us that "Main Street is one of the best places to scout examples of the WDI practice of designing for 'close, medium, and long shots', articulated so well over the years by John Hench. The ideas is that long views establish an idea, medium views continue to support the idea, and close-ups provide elements that reinforce the story. This is why we pay so much attention to details such as carpet patterns, doorknobs, lighting fixtures, and furniture."

- In the *The Imagineering Guide to Disney's Hollywood Studios at Walt Disney World*, Wright explains the role of this practice in bringing stories to life in the parks. "Details such as [this pedestal lantern] help to achieve our goal of consistency in close, medium, and long shots. This reference to filmmaking technique, when applied to our park design, means that each and every detail reinforces the initial view that we have when we are introduced to a new thing. We strive to never blow the illusion when you make your way up close and get a better look."

Examples of this technique can be found throughout all Disney parks, but some specific examples include Cinderella Castle in the

Magic Kingdom, the Tree of Life at Animal Kingdom, and The Twilight Zone Tower of Terror at Hollywood Studios. We're going to look at these three in the next chapter as examples of another technique in the Imagineering Pyramid, but for now our focus will be on how these attractions employ long, medium, and close shots. Increasing levels of detail help guide the audience into their story. You're guided from the general (a castle, a tree, a hotel) to the specific (Cinderella Castle, the Tree of Life, or the Hollywood Tower Hotel). We've already looked at Cinderella Castle earlier; now let's look at these other two examples in more detail.

You first see the Tree of Life at Animal Kingdom as you come around one side or the other of the Oasis. On first glance it appears to be simply a large tree, with a massive trunk at its base and a wide green canopy above. As you approach the tree, the gnarled details of the trunk come into view, as do the thousands of broad green leaves that comprise the canopy. This is clearly a proud and ancient tree, one with a history waiting to be learned. As you approach even closer, the images of countless animals of all shapes and sizes emerge from the trunk and branches. This is truly a "tree of life", imbued with and embodying life of all kinds, a living celebration of the animal kingdom.

As you enter Sunset Boulevard at Hollywood Studios, the Twilight Zone Tower of Terror stands at the far end, beckoning you. From a distance, the building stands out as an old, dilapidated tower, a shadow of its former glory. Moving closer, the extent of the damage becomes more clear, as holes in the walls and remnants of missing portions of the building come into view. Finally, as you walk up along the walkways and into the hotel lobby, the full story of this place comes into focus, with its deserted hallways, dusty and cobwebbed furniture. This is not just any hotel. It's a place that has known tragedy and mystery, and one that invites you to explore its secrets.

Organizing Your Message

As noted above, this technique is about arranging and organizing details to help lead your audience into your experience. To be more specific, it's about *organizing your message to lead your audience from general to the specific*, and involves organizing your details in such a way as to introduce and then support your subject matter.

A basic and familiar example of this practice can be found in the fundamentals of writing a paragraph. The first sentence is a topic sentence that defines the subject of the paragraph. The sentences that follow provide additional detail that support the topic.

Using establishing shots is an effective means of providing context for your audience before drilling down into the details. Without the proper context, your ideas are limited in their ability to effectively convey your message. Ideas without a foundation or connection to other ideas are isolated, and that isolation can limit their potential. Consider the old phrase, "You're missing the forest for trees." This is another way of saying you're so focused on details that you are missing the big picture.

For projects that communicate or convey a message of some sort, such as in the case of a presentation, a marketing campaign, or a book, this practice is essential in organizing your content. It's why so many books begin with an introductory chapter that provides a high-level overview of what the rest of the book contains. Introductions of this sort help provide a starting point for the reader and help establish context for the remainder of the book.

This technique can be also be useful when communicating and promoting your ideas, as a means of organizing your message. For example, if you are presenting information about a new policy or procedure, you wouldn't want to start your presentation with the individual steps of the new procedure. You would start with an overview or introduction (an establishing shot) of the topic (your story) to provide context for your audience. Once they understand the general concept, you can drill down to specific supporting details, such as individual steps or tasks related to the procedure or policy.

In his book *101 Things I Learned in Architecture School*, Matthew Fredrick devotes one of his "101 things" to this practice, writing:

> An effective oral presentation of a studio project begins with the general and proceeds to the specific.
>
> 1. State the design problem assigned.
> 2. Discuss the values, attitude, and approach you brought to the design problem.
> 3. Describe your design process and the major discoveries and ideas you encountered along the way.

4. State the parti, or unifying concept, that emerged from your process. Illustrate this with a simple diagram.
5. Present your drawings (plans, sections, elevations, and vignettes) and models, always describing them in relationship to the parti.
6. Perform a modest and confident self-critique.

Never begin a presentation by saying, "Well, you go in the front door here," unless your goal is to put your audience to sleep.

The Pyramid in Practice—Long, Medium, and Close Up Shots

I've used this practice (or tried to) in every chapter of this book. In each chapter, the opening paragraph provides an establishing shot of the chapter's topic, while the subsequent paragraphs provide medium and close-up details that support and illustrate that topic.

Post-Show: Imagineering Checklist

Using Long, Medium, and Close Shots means *organizing your message to lead your audience from general to the specific*. Long views establish an idea, medium views continue to support the idea, and close-ups provide elements that reinforce the story.

- What is your establishing shot?
- What is your medium shot?
- What is your close up?
- How do your close-up details support your establishing shot?

CHAPTER TEN
Wienies

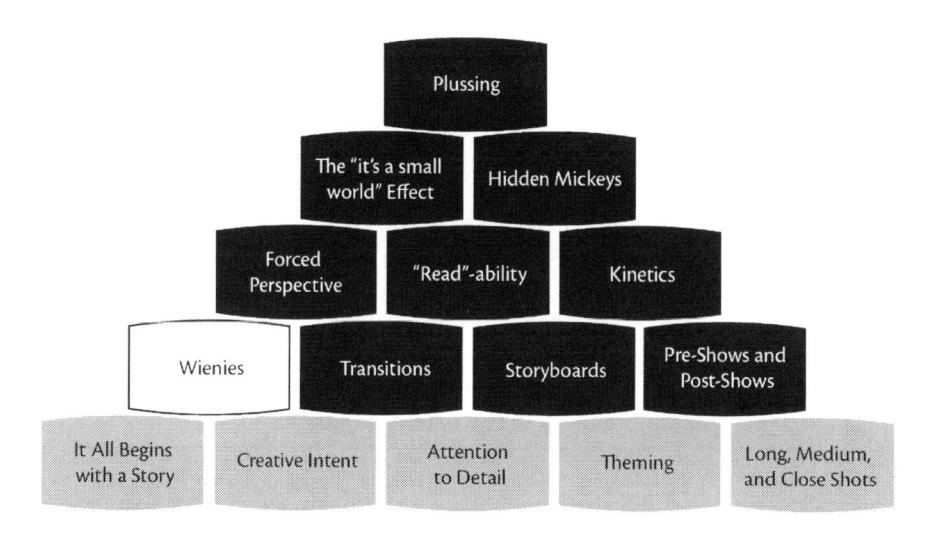

In the last chapter we looked at Cinderella Castle (Magic Kingdom), the Tree of Life (Animal Kingdom), and the Twilight Zone Tower of Terror (Hollywood Studios) as examples of long, medium, and close shots. These three attractions are also examples of another well-known Imagineering practice, one that has its origins with Walt Disney himself. In this chapter we're moving up to the Wayfinding tier in the Imagineering Pyramid which contains principles and practices focused on guiding and leading the audience. The first of these is the use of wienies.

According to Alex Wright, in *The Imagineering Field Guide to Magic Kingdom at Walt Disney World*, the word "wienie" was coined by Walt Disney as a "playful term for a visual element that could be used to draw people into and around a space. A wienie is big enough to be seen from a distance and interesting enough to make you want to take a closer look, like Cinderella Castle at the end of Main Street, U.S.A., or the Astro Orbiter in Tomorrowland." In *How to Be Like Walt*, Pat Williams writes: "During the design phase, Walt told his designers, what you need is a wienie, which says to people 'come this way'. People won't go down a long corridor unless there's something promising at the end. You have to have something that beckons them."

Let's look at how Walt employed wienies at Disneyland from the point of view of a guest entering the park. After buying their ticket, the first wienie guests see is the train station. They then walk through the tunnels beneath the train station, past attraction posters (which we'll get back to in a bit), before emerging in Town Square. At the far end of Main Street sits another wienie, Sleeping Beauty Castle, drawing audiences toward the hub. Once at the hub, there are wienies in all directions. Looking to the left guests see the *Mark Twain* Riverboat, looking to the right they see the Astro Jets (now Astro Orbitor), and looking straight ahead, through Sleeping Beauty Castle, they see the King Arthur Carrousel. Each of these (the train station, Sleeping Beauty Castle, the *Mark Twain*, the Star Jets, and the carrousel) all capture the audience's attention and interest, drawing them to different areas of the park.

In a section devoted to wienies in *Designing Disney*, John Hench notes: "Imagineers have found that people respond to a wienie at the end of a corridor because it beckons them to continue further in their journey.... The wienie promises that you will be rewarded for the time and effort it takes to walk down that corridor.... The Matterhorn at Disneyland, the Tree of Life at Disney's Animal Kingdom, and Big Tillie, the stranded ship at Typhoon Lagoon, are all effective wienies: they set the stage, establish a mood, and draw the eye."

Other well-known Disney park wienies include:
- Cinderella Castle at Magic Kingdom
- Space Mountain at the far end of Tomorrowland in Magic Kingdom and Disneyland
- Big Thunder Mountain and Splash Mountain in Frontierland in Magic Kingdom
- Spaceship Earth at the entrance to Epcot
- The large reddish orb that draws guests into the entry point of the queue of Mission: SPACE at Epcot

- The Twilight Zone Tower of Terror at Hollywood Studios and Disney California Adventure
- The AT-AT Walker outside of Star Tours at Hollywood Studios
- The Tree of Life at Animal Kingdom
- Expedition Everest viewed across Discovery Lake at Animal Kingdom

All of these serve to entice guests to invest their effort to move closer and learn more.

Wienies are often designed as part of the "long shots" described in the previous chapter. For example, Cinderella Castle, the Tree of Life, and the Twilight Zone Tower of Terror are not only examples of long, medium, and close Shots, but are also all wienies in their own right. As John Hench describes, "For a wienie to be effective, we have to set the scene for it, using staging technique derived from film, such as an establishing 'long shot', and special effects and lighting. A long shot in this sense is an intriguing distant view that tells guests where they can go from where they are, promising an adventure, activity, or event."

Wienies also often incorporate movement, or kinetics, something we will be looking at in more detail in a later chapter. Movement on or near a wienie helps catch the audience's eye, drawing their attention and interest to the wienie, which in turn beckons them to take a closer look. Examples of this include the opening doors near the top of the Twilight Zone Tower of Terror that reveal the rising and falling elevator cars, the tea trains climbing the rails between the peaks of Expedition Everest, and the flume boats plummeting down the big drop of Splash Mountain.

The Imagineers also use other visual elements to draw guest attention to attractions in the parks. Remember when I mentioned those attraction posters in the tunnels beneath the train station in Magic Kingdom and Disneyland? While not wienies in the traditional sense, these posters function as a different type of wienie, enticing guests to visit the thrilling attractions that await them within the parks. As Danny Handke and Vanessa Hunt write in *Poster Art of the Disney Parks*, "[C]olorful posters in this lobby entice, excite, and educate guests with a preview of the adventures and experiences inside the Park."

As originally conceived by Walt Disney, wienies are most often visual, but that is not always the case. The Imagineers also create wienies that appeal to other senses. For example, when approaching

Test Track at Epcot, the roar of cars racing around the track serves as an "audio wienie", and when walking near the Main Street Bakery on Main Street, U.S.A. at Magic Kingdom, the smell of fresh baked cookies serves as an "aromatic wienie".

Audience Attention and Interest

Both inside and outside Disney parks, wienies are the same thing: *attracting your audience's attention and capturing their interest*. Anything that serves to grab your audience's attention and capture their interest in learning more about your project can be thought of as a wienie.

Signs and marquees are obvious examples of wienies in the world beyond the berm. Other examples include logos and other graphic design elements used in marketing materials and websites. Graphic design wienies often employ evocative imagery that tells part of the story and entices the audience to learn more. Anytime you find yourself wanting to learn more about a business or product based on its logo, website, or other promotional materials, it's because of the power of wienies at work.

Book covers are another excellent example of wienies at work. A well-designed book cover stands out on a bookstore shelf and not only attracts your attention, but also entices you to pick it up and learn more about what's inside. Wienie-like book cover design encompasses not only the front cover, but also the spine (most books are shelved spine-out on bookstore shelves) and the back cover. Back cover text, including a description of the book as well as possibly snippets from reviewers, can be just as effective as a strong cover image in encouraging readers to crack the cover.

And while wienies tend to be visually based, effective use of language can also serve as a form of wienie. For example, once you've opened a book, textual or verbal wienies can help you make the decision whether or not to buy and read the book. For example, a well-structured table of contents with evocative chapter titles can work as a wienie, as it hopefully captures your attention and encourages you to read the book. Other types of verbal wienies are found on social media networks such as Twitter or Facebook. These social media outlets are filled with verbal wienies in the form of short tag lines and text snippets used to attract readers to follow a link to an article, blog post, or other online content.

For projects that communicate or convey a message of some sort—such as training or teaching materials, a marketing campaign, or a book—using evocative language when first introducing concepts to your audience can entice them to invest the time to learn more. When communicating and promoting your project, use words and phrases that subtly suggest what your project is about, without giving it all away. This will help encourage your audience to want to learn more.

The Pyramid in Practice—Wienies

I've tried to use creative and catchy names for many of the principles described in this book so that those names will act as wienies for readers. My hope is that names such as "Read"-ability, The "it's a small world" Effect, and Plussing are intriguing enough to encourage you to want to learn more. Beyond their names, I hope the short descriptions of each principle in my overview of the Imagineering Pyramid (in chapter 2) provide just enough of a hint about what each entails that you will want to read the corresponding chapters.

Post-Show: Imagineering Checklist

Wienies are used in *attracting your audience's attention and capturing their interest.*

- What type of wienie makes sense for your project? Should you use visual wienies, verbal wienies, or both?
- Are you using creative language to entice your audience to want to learn more about your project?
- Are you using effective graphic design to capture your audience's attention and interest?

CHAPTER ELEVEN
Transitions

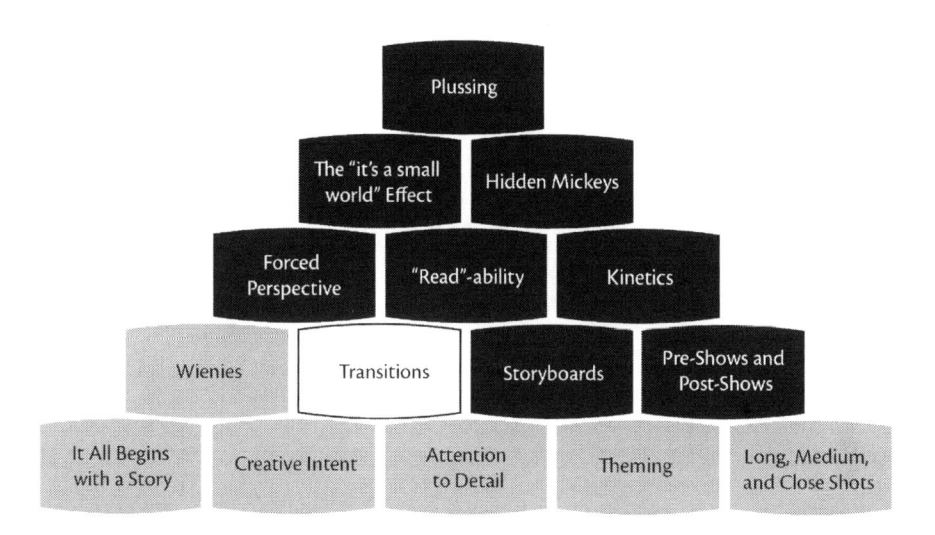

We've just looked at wienies and how they're used in the parks to draw guests toward and into specific experiences. Guests often move from one land to another, such as when leaving the hub to enter Frontierland, Adventureland, Fantasyland, or Tomorrowland at Disneyland, or when leaving Liberty Square and entering Frontierland on the way toward Splash Mountain in Magic Kingdom. As they do so, the theming, colors, textures, walkways, and even background music (BGM) around them changes subtly, and before they know it they're in a completely different environment. This subtle and often overlooked experience is the next block in the Wayfinding tier of the Imagineering Pyramid, and is a technique called Transitions.

Transitions involve making sure that as guests make their way through the park, the changes they experience as they move from subject to subject, or area to area, are as seamless as possible. The Imagineers accomplish this through the use of what the they call "three-dimensional cross-dissolves" that employ different sorts of sensory cues to let their audience know that they're moving to a different area. In her obituary for John Hench on MousePlanet.com, Sheila Hagen notes Hench's "...philosophy was that the parks were like movies, and the designer must provide transitions between one 'scene' to another; gradual changes in color and design helped to avoid making the changes abrupt. He did this most often through his legendary gift of color sense." In his book *Designing Disney*, John Hench describes this technique, saying that "[Walt] had us provide provide guests with subtle sensory clues that indicate change is happening. As guests walk from Main Street into Adventureland, walkway surfaces change from concrete to cut stone, wrought-iron hand railings give way to bamboo, Main Street's music yields to growls and howls."

Another detailed example of how the Imagineers use transitions can be found in *The Imagineering Field Guide to the Magic Kingdom*:

> The transitions from land to land in our parks are always carefully considered, but the one from Fantasyland to Liberty Square—or Liberty Square to Fantasyland, depending on your point of view—is one of the most successful. The transition takes its cues from the standard film cross-dissolve. In order to make your way from one land to the other, you must pass beneath an overpass, actually a seating area in the Columbia Harbor House. There are elements from each land that appear on each side of the pass-through. You'll see stonework reminiscent of the castle wall in Liberty Square, and Tudor-style woodwork on both sides of the restaurant. Your view narrows and goes dark as you travel through the tunnel, and there is even a separate BGM track playing in this space to complete the dissolve. It's one of the finest and subtlest moments in your walk in the Park.

Transitions are also used between scenes within attractions and shows. In describing the World of Color show at Disney California Adventure, Alex Wright explains that "[g]reat care is taken in establishing the transitions between sequences, so that one flows seamlessly into the next. Color and movement and even relationships between content and even subject matter in adjacent scenes are used to establish these connections. The end result is a compendium show that maintains its own internal thread of logic."

Further examples of attraction transitions are found in an article entitled "Pirates of the Caribbean ... More Gems from This Disney Treasure" in issue 32 of *The "E" Ticket* magazine:

> The contrast between the somber settings of the Grotto and the lusty action of the Spanish town reinforces and reminds us of the framework of logic within Pirates of the Caribbean ... the "layers of fantasy" established by the ride's designers to help shape reality for the audience in a credible way, and in stages. Some of these layers are obvious, like the change from day to night, or from the Anaheim locale to New Orleans, then the Caribbean. Others are dramatic, like the illusion of being inside, then outside (Blue Bayou outside, inside the grotto, battle scene outside, etc.) and the elegant contrast in atmosphere which results. Less apparent are the transitions which help the audience accept and adjust to the surprises still to come. In the Grotto, the first pirate skeletons are shown undisturbed where they lay. Further along, the skeletons are engaged in more "lively" pursuits like steering the ship or gulping rum at the bar. Deeper in the caves, the dead pirates seem as if still alive, reviewing treasure maps or fondling treasure. This shift from the realistic to the whimsical helps prepare the audience for adventures even more fantastic further along in the attraction.

Smooth and Seamless Change

Transitions are all about *making change as smooth and seamless as possible*. As your audience moves through your experience, you want ideas and concepts to flow as smoothly as possible from one to the next. One of the tools we'll discuss later—Storyboards—can be used when planning and designing transitions; other tools such as Theming and "Read"-ability can be helpful when implementing your transitions.

The same types of transitions as are found in Disney parks are also found in other art forms as well. One example is in the design of video games in which transitions are used to help smooth the changes that players experience as they progress through the game. A specific example of this is Disney's *Epic Mickey* game for the Wii console. As Austin Grossman describes in *The Art of Epic Mickey*:

> The world is full of dark purples and greens, and levels of Disney's *Epic Mickey* each have their own palette. As players advance through the game, they move through a carefully planned series of color schemes that ease the transition between the different parts of Wasteland, so that the changes aren't too jarring. The shifts in color also create a kind of visual storyline for the game.

Transitions also have a role in other, perhaps less obvious fields. One of my favorite TV shows is *Face Off*, a competition and elimination series focused on special-effects makeup. When the series judges evaluate the contestants' makeups, they often focus on transitions within a makeup, implemented through changes in paint color, sculptural texture, costuming, and other effects. These transitions take place between different areas of a makeup, such as from the model's chest up through their neck and face, or from the model's hands up to their arms and chest, and even transitions between prosthetics and skin.

Most transitions are designed to allow for smooth change between scenes, but there are times when an abrupt change is more appropriate. In these cases, the Imagineers use a "crash cut"—a filmmaking term used to denote an abrupt transition. For example, the end scene in Journey into Imagination with Figment features an abrupt change in which the set changes entirely during a brief blackout (another tool in the Imagineers' transition toolkit). This transition is abrupt by design. When used sparingly, crash cuts can keep your experience dynamic.

Like wienies, transitions can take non-visual forms. For instance, when presenting information, consider the transitions between topics when determining the "best" order and sequence in which topics should be addressed. These transitions should be designed so that information flows smoothly and doesn't jump randomly from topic to topic.

The Pyramid in Practice—Transitions

Transitions played a role when I was outlining and writing this book. I went through several iterations of the order of the chapters in this book before I settled on the final version.

Post-Show: Imagineering Checklist

Transitions are used in *making change as smooth and seamless as possible*.

- Are there specific tools you can use to help create effective transitions in your project?
- Are you avoiding abrupt changes within your experience?
- Are you guiding your audience from subject to subject in a manner that helps them understand?
- Have you considered the order in which you're presenting your ideas? Do they flow smoothly, or do they jump around?

CHAPTER TWELVE
Storyboards

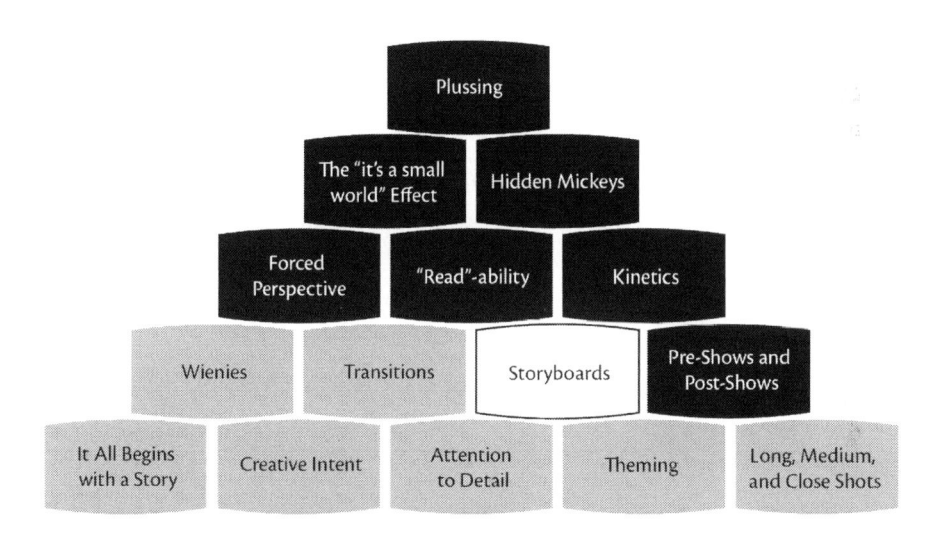

You can find examples of most of the principles in the Imagineering Pyramid as you walk around Disney theme parks. We've already looked at examples of Transitions, Wienies, and Long, Medium, and Close Shots, as well as examples of how an attraction's story and Creative Intent can be seen through the use of Theming and Attention to Detail. The next principle in the Wayfinding tier of the Imagineering Pyramid is one of only a very few practices and tools of which examples aren't found in the Disney parks—Storyboards.

Storyboards are large pin-up boards used to post ideas, or to outline the story points of a ride or film. Each story point or idea is on an individual sheet of paper or card. These allow designers to see the entire sequence of events in a story or ride, and re-arrange them as needed during development.

Walt Disney popularized the use of storyboards in the development of animated films. Because many of the first Imagineers came from Disney's Animation Department, they borrowed this technique when designing Disneyland. As Pat Williams describes in *How To Be Like Walt*: "Walt insisted on storyboarding every project—not just cartoons. Walt used storyboards to plan every shot of his live-action films and every thrill of his Disneyland attractions." The Imagineers use storyboards to plot out the experience that their guests will have when they visit Disney theme parks and attractions.

Storyboards are developed in detail during the formal design stage of the Imagineering process, setting the stage for more detailed design of each scene within an attraction. The Imagineers also use storyboards when initially developing and fleshing out ideas during the early blue sky and concept development stages as well. As John Hench says, in *Designing Disney*, "Storyboards enable us to design sequences of experiences that take guests to peak moments."

The *Imagineering Field Guide* series is a good source of examples of storyboard art used in the design of Disney theme park attractions, including:

- Cars Land and Monsters, Inc.: Mike & Sulley to the Rescue! (Disney California Adventure)
- Roger Rabbit's Car Toon Spin and Finding Nemo Submarine Voyage (Disneyland)
- DINOSAUR (Animal Kingdom)
- Fantastmic! (Hollywood Studios)

Seeing the Big Picture

Storyboards are about *seeing the big picture*, and are used primarily to help visualize and plot out the sequence of events in a story, attraction, or other project. In addition, storyboards can be used when designing and planning transitions within your experience (which we looked at in the last chapter).

While traditional storyboards are most often sketches and illustrations, any format or tool that helps you step back and see the larger picture of what you're creating can be thought of as a storyboard. For example, in instructional design you can use storyboards to outline the entire classroom experience (including lectures, quizzes, and exercises) and as a visual tool to "see" the entire course. You might use three different colors of index cards for different types of content (white = lecture, green = quiz, blue = exercise), with each card containing a title or phrase describing each piece of the course. By putting those on a board and looking at it from a distance, you can see if you have too much of one type of content vs another ("We have too much lecture here, we should spread this out...." etc.).

Storyboarding can be done with a physical storyboard or with computer-based storyboarding tools. There are several stand-alone storyboard applications available (just Google "storyboard software"), and storyboard tools are also included in some writing applications as well. One example of this is Scrivener, the application I'm using to write this book. Scrivener includes a corkboard feature that allows users to view different chapters and topics as note cards on a cork board which can be shuffled and re-arranged as needed.

Another technique and concept similar to storyboarding is mind mapping, which employs diagrams to organize and display information in a visual manner (sound familiar?). Like storyboards, mind mapping can be done manually (often on a white board or flip chart) or using software tools that allow you to quickly and easily move elements around within an outline or a map. I use mind maps when outlining nearly everything I do, including the initial outline of this book.

Storyboarding is also used in business as a brainstorming/ideation technique in strategic planning sessions. In a common form of this, participants are asked to write down ideas on individual index cards which are then posted on a board so everyone involved can see them all. The cards can then be rearranged and placed in related groups. In some practices, participants also "vote" on ideas by placing small colored stickers (dots) on individual cards. Ideas receiving the most votes are prioritized above those receiving fewer votes.

The Pyramid in Practice—Storyboards

As I noted above, I used a storyboard/mind map when outlining this book. I moved several items around during the outlining phase, and using a mind map made it much easier for me to step back and visualize the entire book.

Post-Show: Imagineering Checklist

Storyboards entail *seeing the big picture* and can be used to *visualize and plot out the sequence of events in a story, attraction, or other project.* Mind mapping can be used as a form of storyboarding. Storyboarding can also be used as a brainstorming/ideation technique.

- Are using storyboards or a mind map to visualize your project?
- Have you stepped back to "see" your entire project?
- Have you considered different ways in which to arrange the pieces of your project?

CHAPTER THIRTEEN
Pre-Shows and Post-Shows

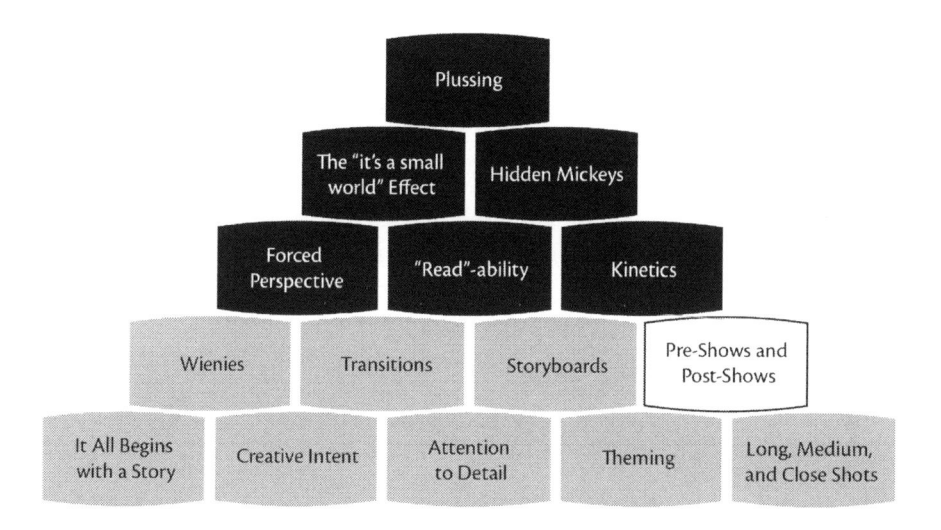

When you experience a Disney theme park attraction, it's uncommon that you do so without some form of introduction before the attraction or a reminder after it. In fact, nearly all Disney park attractions lead guests into and out of the attraction in some way or another. This practice is the domain of the fourth and last block of the Wayfinding tier of the Imagineering Pyramid, what Imagineers refer to as Pre-Shows and Post-Shows.

Pre-shows prepare the audience for what they are about to experience and often help convey the attraction's creative intent. In the Disney parks, pre-shows are the parts of an attraction that you experience before you enter the attraction itself. In *The Imagineering Guide to Epcot at Walt Disney World*, Alex Wright tells us that "[p]re-shows are very important to WDI, and go a long way toward enhancing an experience for our guests. It can put them into a particular mood or provide them with helpful background information that will ensure that all the elements of the show make sense ... A pre-show, however, can begin before you even get to the doors of an attraction."

Anything you encounter in an attraction's line (or queue) would count as part of its pre-show. In some attractions, pre-shows primarily comprise themed areas like the richly themed queues in the Twilight Zone Tower of Terror or Expedition Everest. Consider how the Expedition Everest pre-show prepares guests for the experience that awaits them. The queue brings guests through a Yeti museum where they see artifacts, legends, and "facts" about the Yeti as well as remnants of previous expeditions to the Forbidden Mountain. The information in the queue sets the stage for the perilous journey they're about to undertake.

In some cases, attraction queues also include interactive activities. Many attractions at Magic Kingdom at Walt Disney World have had interactive elements added to their queues, including the Seven Dwarfs Mine Train, the Many Adventures of Winnie the Pooh, Big Thunder Mountain Railroad, and the Haunted Mansion. Pre-shows can also include short films that provide a sneak peak of what you will experience on the attraction. The Twilight Zone Tower of Terror makes use of this via the short video introduction to the episode of *The Twilight Zone* that you're about to star in. Another good example of this is Mission: SPACE at Epcot, in which you watch a short film that explains the mission you're about to undertake and even provides some basic training information about your role in that mission.

Post-shows reinforce key ideas and themes, and most often include themed areas or interactive activities or games. Going back to *The Imagineering Field Guide to Epcot at Walt Disney World*: "Mission: SPACE offers a great illustration of a post-show. Post-show spaces extend the themes of a show beyond the attraction itself, allowing the experience to continue for those who have ridden the attraction, or begin for those who bypassed the ride. Post-shows can take on many formats. This one [Mission: SPACE] is focused on interactive experiences and group games that build on the stories of space exploration and teamwork that are the centerpiece of the ride-adventure."

Other examples of post-show activities at Epcot include Spaceship Earth and The Seas with Nemo and Friends. The Spaceship Earth post-show includes a number of activities that you can try out as you exit the attraction that relate to ideas you learned about during the attraction. The post-show at The Seas with Nemo & Friends (originally known as Seabase Alpha) is a large aquarium exhibit and a number of other smaller sea life exhibits.

One other form of post-show is what's referred to in the themed entertainment world as "exit through retail" in which guests are led through a themed merchandise shop as they exit an attraction. Examples of this include Space Mountain and Mickey's Philharmagic at Magic Kingdom; Rock 'n' Roller Coaster, Star Tours, and the Twilight Zone Tower of Terror at Hollywood Studios; Mission: SPACE at Epcot; and Expedition Everest and DINOSAUR at Animal Kingdom. You might question whether merchandise would qualify as a post-show, but consider that a souvenir such as a key chain or t-shirt can help you remember the experience you had on an attraction long after you've left the park. In my view, that's as valid a post-show as any other. Plus, these are post-shows that you can take home!

Introducing and Reinforcing Concepts

There is a well-known saying in the realm of public speaking and giving presentations that has its origins with Aristotle, and goes something like this: "Tell them what you're going to tell them, tell them, then tell them what you told them." This is what pre-shows and post-shows are all about: *introducing and reinforcing your story to help your audience get and stay engaged*. Disney park pre-shows are specifically designed to set the stage for what the guests are going to experience and lead the audience into the experience, and post-shows are designed to follow up on key ideas in the attraction. Whenever possible, you should do the same thing when communicating your story to your audience.

When presenting information to an audience, jumping directly into your message without some form of introduction can confuse them since they have no context for what you're telling them. Likewise, ending a presentation without some form of review can lead your audience to forget the key points of your message. When giving a presentation, starting with an overview (a pre-show) that outlines what you're going to share with your audience sets the stage for your presentation and prepares your audience for what's to come (your overview can also serve as a wienie). Similarly, ending your presentation with a review (a post-show) of the information you've covered helps to reinforce your ideas. A classic example of using pre-shows and post-shows in presentations often takes the form of an Introduction/Overview/Agenda slide at the beginning of your presentation that highlights your main topics ("Today we're going to talk about..."), and a Review slide at the end of the presentation that reiterates those same main topics ("To review, we've talked about..."). While this approach may seem hackneyed or even cliched, it is effective.

The form that your pre-shows and post-shows take will vary depending on the nature of your project. Just as anything guests encounter in an attraction's queue is part of its pre-show, your pre-show can be anything you're able to do to introduce your ideas to your audience. It can include announcements, promotional items, or anything designed to introduce your audience to your subject matter. As an example, if you're planning a meeting or information session in your workplace, your pre-show might be as simple as an email to attendees that outlines the goals of the meeting. Likewise, your post-shows can take different forms. In the meeting example above, your post-show can be as simple as a follow-up email that summarizes the main points discussed at the meeting, or could be detailed meeting minutes.

Let's look at an example of how pre-shows and post-shows are used in a current business practice. Many companies today offer free webinars (web-based seminars) that present audiences with ideas, concepts, and tools they can use in their businesses. To spread the word about these events, announcements are sent out via email and social media to prospective attendees. These announcements (pre-shows) typically contain an introduction and overview of the webinar, and what attendees can expect to learn. Then, following the webinar, the presenter or sponsoring organization will often post or email links to presentation materials or recordings of the webinar. These follow-up emails (post-shows) and presentation materials serve to remind attendees of what they learned.

If your project is one that communicates or conveys a message of some sort (such as a marketing campaign or training course), you should include pre-shows and post-shows as a part of your design. Pre-shows and post-shows are also useful when communicating and promoting your ideas.

The Pyramid in Practice— Pre-Shows and Post-Shows

Part One of this book is intended to serve as the book's pre-show, providing a high-level overview of what's to come in the following chapters. The final chapter takes a look back and serves as a post-show. In addition, post-show sections in most chapters summarize and highlight key ideas from the chapter.

Post-Show: Imagineering Checklist

Pre-shows and post-shows are a means of *introducing and reinforcing your story to help your audience stay engaged*. They can take different forms, depending on the nature of your subject matter and your project.

- What is your pre-show? How are you introducing your subject matter to your audience?
- Do you have a post-show? How are you reinforcing your subject matter for your audience?

CHAPTER FOURTEEN
Forced Perspective

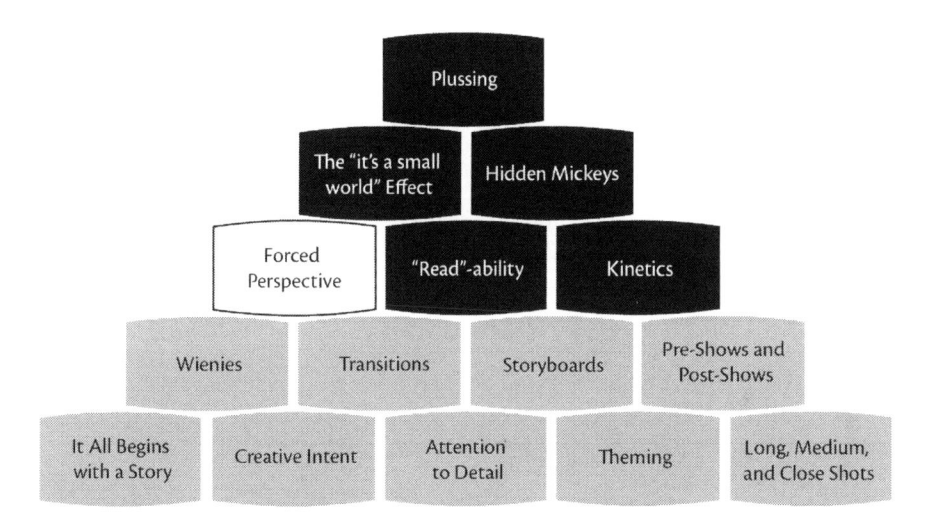

```
                    Plussing
        The "it's a small
           world" Effect        Hidden Mickeys
     Forced
   Perspective      "Read"-ability      Kinetics
                                              Pre-Shows and
  Wienies        Transitions      Storyboards    Post-Shows
 It All Begins                    Attention                Long, Medium,
  with a Story   Creative Intent  to Detail    Theming    and Close Shots
```

The third tier in the Imagineering Pyramid includes principles and techniques related primarily to visual communication. These techniques are used throughout Disney parks in different ways, and you can find examples of them in nearly every land and attraction. The first technique, Forced Perspective, is all about the illusion of size.

Forced perspective is a technique where by the designer plays with scale in order to affect the perception of the audience. Through use of forced perspective, structures or objects can appear larger or smaller than they really are. Forced perspective has its origins as a theatrical technique, and is another principle that the early Imagineers borrowed from their previous roles as art directors and animators.

Forced perspective can be found in a number of places in the parks. One prime example is on Main Street, U.S.A. at Walt Disney World's

Magic Kingdom, where the first floor facades are built at 90% of full size, the second floor facades at 80%, and the third floor facades slightly smaller still. As you walk past these structures, you think you're walking past three-story buildings, but they're really not three stories tall. This same technique is used in a number of other places, including Cinderella Castle and the Twilight Zone Tower of Terror. Other examples of forced perspective include:

- Disneyland's Frontierland where, explains Alex Wright in *The Imagineering Field Guide to Disneyland*, "the plant palette makes use of a type of forced perspective to enhance the feeling of space, bringing the larger species within close proximity of our guests, and placing smaller, closer-planter varieties farther away".
- Disneyland's New Orleans Square and Main Street, U.S.A., where the buildings and facades are scaled down.
- Space Mountain at Disneyland and Magic Kingdom, where beams on the outside of the building create forced perspective on the exterior as the columns converge toward the top of the building.
- World Showcase pavilions at Epcot including Hotel du Canada and the Rocky Mountains at the Canada Pavilion, the Eiffel Tower in the France Pavilion, the Campinale in the Italy Pavilion, and the pyramid at the Mexico Pavilion.

Though typically used to make things look larger than they are, forced perspective can also be used to make things appear smaller. For example, the American Adventure Pavilion at Epcot is designed to look like a Colonial building, but due to issues of crowd control and capacity, the building is much larger than any building from Colonial times. To address this, the Imagineers use forced perspective in a "reverse" way to make the building seem smaller. The building is actually nearly five stories tall, but appears to be just over two stories.

Another good example of forced perspective is Snow White's Grotto in Fantasyland at Disneyland. At one point, Walt Disney commissioned a set of statues of Snow White and the Seven Dwarfs from an Italian sculptor, but when the statues arrived, the Imagineers discovered that all of the statues were the same size. Snow White was the same size as the dwarfs. As a result, the statues couldn't be placed next to each other. John Hench came up with the idea of putting Snow White toward the back of the display and using forced perspective to create the illusion that she's actually bigger than the dwarfs.

In addition to making elements in the parks look larger or smaller than they really are, Imagineers also use differences in scale to make things look farther away. As Alex Wright notes in *The Imagineering Field Guide to Disney California Adventure*, "there are other ways to trick the eye. Color, too, can come into play to imply distance. As objects get farther away from us, they also tend to become less saturated in color and have less contrast between the highlights and shadows. This is known as atmospheric perspective—an effect that has been put to great use over the years in painting and is evident when you look closely at landscape photography." Some attractions combine forced and atmospheric perspective to create the illusion of both size and distance, such as Expedition Everest at Animal Kingdom. As Alex Wright explains in *The Imagineering Field Guide to Disney's Animal Kingdom at Walt Disney World*: "[A]t the Everest overlook is a map of the range and a telescope that helps guests spot which of the peaks of the attraction actually represents Mount Everest itself. Tricks of forced perspective—in this case atmospheric effects including desaturation of color and diminishing scale of detail—place the mountain far into the distance."

The Illusion of Size

Forced perspective is about *using the illusion of size to help communicate your message*. Any approach you employ to adjust (or force) the perspective of your audience to help them understand your subject matter can be considered forced perspective. Given its origins in theatrical design, forced perspective is most commonly encountered as a visual device, similar to the way the Imagineers use it in the Disney parks, but forced perspective can take different forms, based on your needs.

When communicating ideas, we can leverage different types of forced perspective to make our ideas seem smaller and simpler than they really are (this is also related to the next technique—"Read"-ability). Some specific ways to do this include grouping and chunking. Grouping is useful when dealing with something that involves a large number of small (or at least relatively small) pieces or steps, and simply involves grouping sets of related ideas into a smaller number of sets or groups. For example, if you're trying to explain a process that involves 37 steps, grouping those steps into 4–5 groups of 7–10 steps each can help your audience not feel overwhelmed by the sheer number of steps to perform. Chunking is "a method of presenting information which splits concepts into small pieces or 'chunks' of information to make reading and understanding faster and easier". It's is useful when dealing with large, complex concepts.

The craft of world building found in fantasy and science fiction—as well as in game design—provides an example of another form of forced perspective. Game designer and author Jesse Schell describes an example of this in *The Art of Game Design: A Book of Lenses*: "J.R.R. Tolkien's worlds are famous for being deep and rich—one way he achieves this is through a trick he referred to as 'distant mountains'. Throughout his books, he gives names to distant places, people, and events that are never actually encountered in the book. The names and brief descriptions make it seem like the world is larger and richer than it is." Most, if not all, richly developed fantasy and science fiction universes—including those found in roleplaying and video games—make some use of Tolkien's distant mountains.

The Pyramid in Practice— Forced Perspective

Both the Imagineering Pyramid itself and the tiers that comprise it are examples of my attempts at using forced perspective. Rather than present the principles of the pyramid as a set of 15 individual topics, by arranging them in a pyramid, and in separate tiers (groups) within the pyramid, I'm hoping it helps readers better understand how the different principles are related to each other.

Post-Show: Imagineering Checklist

Forced perspective involves *using the illusion of size to help communicate your message*. Grouping and chunking are specific ways to employ forced perspective when communicating ideas. Forced perspective can take different forms—it need not always be visual.

- Are you trying to adjust your audience's perspective to help communicate your message?
- Are you simplifying large or complex subjects?
- Are using grouping and/or chunking?
- How can you employ Tolkien's distant mountains?

CHAPTER FIFTEEN
"Read"-ability

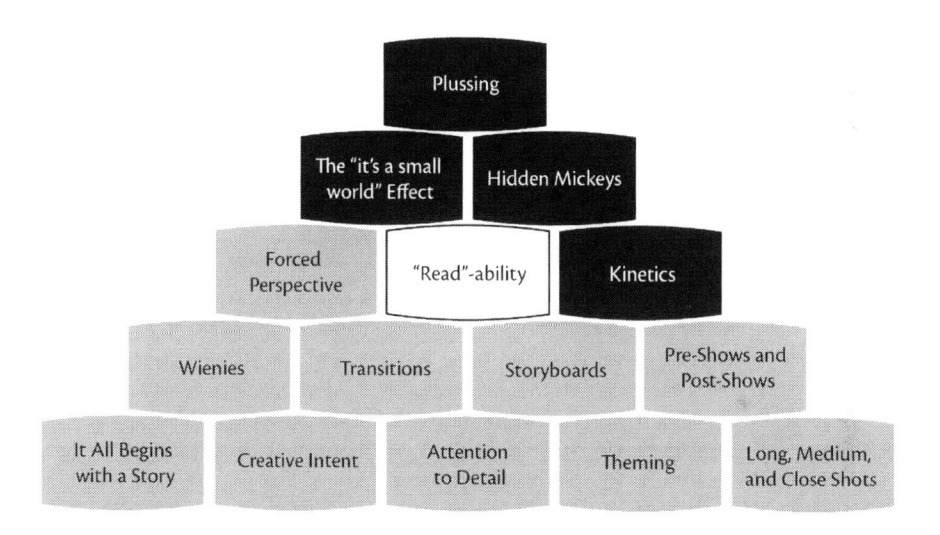

```
                    Plussing
         The "it's a small      Hidden Mickeys
            world" Effect
    Forced              "Read"-ability         Kinetics
  Perspective
                                              Pre-Shows and
   Wienies      Transitions    Storyboards     Post-Shows
It All Begins                   Attention                  Long, Medium,
 with a Story  Creative Intent  to Detail     Theming     and Close Shots
```

The next block in the Imagineering Pyramid sits in the center of the third tier, and is a principle and practice that I call "Read"-ability. This is an important tool in the Imagineers' toolbox, and is used in many different ways in the Disney parks and resorts.

In ride systems, particularly dark rides, guests pass through scenes quickly, and there is only a short time (3–5 seconds) to convey what's happening, so the audience must be able to immediately understand each scene. The Imagineers solve this by creating images or scenes that can be "read" quickly by audiences. Scenes of this type are found in many attractions, but some of the most memorable examples can be found in the Pirates of the Caribbean, including the dunk-the-mayor scene, the wench auction, and perhaps the most famous example of all, the jail scene.

The practice of "read"-ability has its roots in the sight gags of Disney's animated films, and was one of several techniques that Walt's animators brought with them when they joined WED Enterprises. In *The Imagineering Field Guide to Disneyland*, Alex Wright tells us that "[t]he art of the WDI sight gag was perfected by Imagineer Marc Davis. One of Walt's Nine Old Men [of animation], he was known to be one of the finest draftsmen ever to work at the studio. His work for Walt Disney Animation, including the classic characters Tinker Bell, Princess Aurora, and Cruella De Vil, gave him an impeccable sense of timing that allowed his creations to read instantly—an important consideration in light of the limited time and dialog available as the audience moves through a scene."

One of the key tools the Imagineers use in creating readable scenes is the use of appropriate details. As Alex Wright explains: "Little details really do catch our eyes, whether consciously or subconsciously, and instantly become a part of our perception. This information is key to our storytelling, and the way it has to be delivered in a Disney park is unique. We have to communicate these character traits very quickly, as the timing of the show typically doesn't allow the audience to visually explore the scene completely—at least not the first time through."

An article, "Pirates of the Caribbean: More Gems from This Disney Treasure", from issue 32 of *The E-Ticket* offers this example: "One subtle but effective technique is achieved with the use of painted blue-green moonlight and dark grey shadows across the stonework, marking in silhouette the shapes of posts, pillars, steps and barrels. These accented details give depth, help the scene "read" from a distance, and increase the color range between the hot burning buildings and the cooler areas still untouched by flames."

In chapter 10, we talked about how attraction posters can serve as wienies, but attraction posters are also excellent examples of "read"-ability. In *Poster Art of the Disney Parks*, Danny Handke and Vanessa Hunt discuss the role that these posters can play in the guest experience: "[W]hy use posters instead of other advertising media? Posters speak to the audience on the move. They capture the viewer's attention and get the message across in a matter of seconds. Successful posters tell the story quickly, directly, and clearly. It's true that a picture is worth a thousand words, and the first Disneyland attraction posters were no exception."

While "read"-ability is perhaps most often found within attractions, it is also used in other ways in the Disney parks. Specifically, both wienies and long shots need to be readable so that guests can quickly understand them. Examples of readable long shots can be found in World Showcase at Epcot, where the Imagineers designed the pavilions to be readable from a distance. Alex Wright explains: "Besides choosing iconic landmarks that are instantly recognizable in the "long shot", we also limit ourselves to national vernacular building facades in the accompanying streetscapes. This is done to ensure that each country's face portrays a very singular appearance that cannot be mistaken for any other."

Simplification: The Heart of "Read"-ability

"Read"-ability is the practice of *simplifying complex subjects*. Whenever you need to communicate complex (or even not-that-complex) ideas, you should look for ways in which you can simplify your message to help your audience quickly and easily understand what you're trying to tell them.

In *The Art of Explanation: Making Your Ideas, Products, and Services Easier to Understand*, Lee Lefever describes simplification as "transforming complex bundles of details into big, understandable ideas that serve as stepping-stones to understanding". He then follows this definition by offering six approaches to simplification:

- Do not make assumptions about what people already know
- Use the most basic language possible
- Zoom out and try to see the object from the broadest perspective possible
- Forget the details and exceptions and focus on the big idea
- Be willing to trade accuracy for understanding
- Connect the basic ideas to ideas the audience already understands

When you're trying to make your creative projects more "read"-able, step back and consider these six approaches and how you might apply them to your work.

In the realm of theme park attractions, the need for "read"-ability is based on timing and the need to quickly convey a message before the audience moves onto another vignette, but "read"-ability isn't just about speed. It's about *making ideas easily understandable*, which in turn makes them quickly understandable. Even in circumstances when you're not constrained by time, it's still a good idea to consider how to help your audience understand your subject matter.

Examples of "read"-ability in the world beyond the berm can be found in a number of fields, some fairly obvious such as advertising or graphic design, and others perhaps less so. In a previous chapter I mentioned that one of my favorites television shows is *Face Off*, a reality competition and elimination series focused on special-effects makeup. In this show, well-known special-effects makeup artist Michael Westmore serves as the series mentor/consultant and meets with contestants early in the design stages of their tasks. One of the key criteria Westmore discusses during these consultations is if and how well each contestant's make up "reads". For instance, if the artist is creating a werewolf, does the makeup "read" as a werewolf. The judges also often discuss the "read"-ability of the makeups, and as often as not, makeups that don't "read" as they should can lead to contestants being eliminated from the show.

Some of the most effective tools to employ "read"-ability are illustrations, examples, and metaphors. As the saying goes, a picture is worth a thousand words, and photographs, illustrations, and diagrams can go a long way toward simplifying your message. A great example can be found in the instruction books that come with LEGO building sets. LEGO instructions typically have no words, but instead solely use illustrations. The true effectiveness of the LEGO approach to instructions was made vividly clear to me in a training class I attended, in which the class divided into three teams and competed to see which team could assemble a small LEGO set the quickest. Each team was given a different set of instructions. One team used a set of instructions that were entirely text, another used instructions that included text and some illustrations, and the last used standard LEGO instructions—all illustrations. The team with the standard LEGO instructions completed the set in roughly half the time it took my team (the team with the all-text instructions).

Examples are another great tool to assist with "read"-ability, and often help your audience understand your subject matter by placing them within a specific context. In my role as a technical writer, I often use examples to explain how different aspects of our software applications work. Providing business-based examples of certain features helps readers understand how they can use those features in their own business. You likely can't help but notice that I cite examples of each of the principles of the Imagineering Pyramid in each chapter. That's because rather than relying just on my words to explain these concepts, the examples help more effectively communicate the message.

Lastly, metaphors can be an effective means of simplifying your subject matter. In his book *I Is an Other: The Secret Life of Metaphor and How It Shapes the Way We See the World*, James Geary tells us: "Metaphorical thinking—our instinct not just for describing but for comprehending one thing in terms of another, for equating I with an other—shapes our view of the world, and is essential to how we communicate, learn, discover, and invent." Finding an appropriate and effective metaphor can be challenging, but can reap huge rewards in terms of conveying your subject matter effectively and efficiently.

I recently came across a great metaphor for the challenges faced in many businesses in a book entitled *Orbiting the Giant Hairball: A Corporate Fool's Guide to Surviving with Grace* by Gordon MacKenzie, who uses the metaphor of the "giant hairball' to represent the morass of business decisions, policies, and procedures that make many businesses inefficient. Related to this is the idea of "orbiting the hairball". As MacKenzie describes it: "Orbiting is responsible creativity: vigorously exploring and operating beyond the Hairball of the corporate mind set, beyond "accepted models, patterns, or standards"—all the while remaining connected to the spirit of the corporate mission. To find Orbit around a corporate Hairball is to find a place of balance where you benefit from the physical, intellectual, and philosophical resources of the organization without becoming entombed in the bureaucracy of the institution."

For anyone working in a creative field (and that's all of us, right?), this metaphor aptly conveys the struggle and balance we face when employing our creativity while having to deal with deep-rooted (though perhaps well-intentioned) corporate bureaucracy.

The Pyramid in Practice—"Read"-ability

"Read"-ability is the principle that gave birth to this book, and appropriately enough, it's in the center of the pyramid. This whole book is an exercise in "read"-ability. The craft of Imagineering is a complex one, but I've tried to make it easier to understand by identifying specific principles and practices used by the Imagineers.

Post-Show: Imagineering Checklist

"Read"-ability is about *simplifying complex subjects,* and *making ideas easily understandable*. Illustrations, examples, and metaphors are helpful tools in employing "read"-ability.

- Are you simplifying complex ideas?
- How can you make your subject matter more "read"-able?
- Are you using illustrations, examples, or metaphors to help explain your subject matter?

CHAPTER SIXTEEN
Kinetics

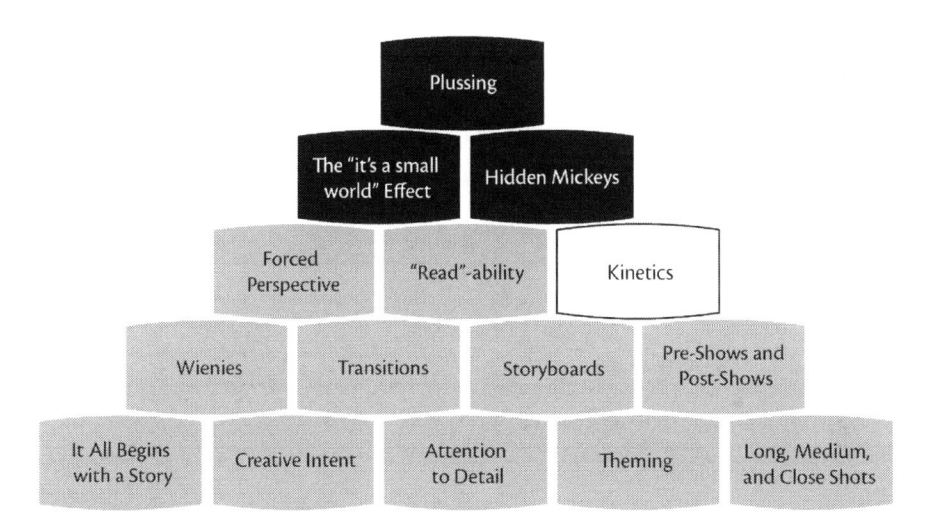

Pyramid diagram with tiers:
- Plussing
- The "it's a small world" Effect | Hidden Mickeys
- Forced Perspective | "Read"-ability | Kinetics
- Wienies | Transitions | Storyboards | Pre-Shows and Post-Shows
- It All Begins with a Story | Creative Intent | Attention to Detail | Theming | Long, Medium, and Close Shots

The third and final block in the middle tier of the Imagineering Pyramid is called Kinetics, a term that, according to Alex Wright in *The Imagineering Field Guide to Magic Kingdom at Walt Disney World*, Disney Imagineers use to describe "[m]ovement and motion in a scene that give it life and energy. This can come from moving vehicles, active signage, changes in the lighting, special effects, or even hanging banners or flags that move around as the wind blows."

Like many of the techniques and tools used by the Imagineers, Kinetics has ties back to the studio's origins in animation. In animation, kinetics is born from animated figures moving in front of (mostly) static backgrounds. As animator and Imagineer Rolly Crump explains: "Your eye watches what moves. When you've got an animated screen going, or when you've got an animated cartoon on the screen, you're not looking at the backgrounds." The same holds true in the three-dimensional world of Disney theme parks.

There are few truly "still" places in the Disney theme parks. The Imagineers use kinetics to keep the atmosphere in the parks alive, dynamic, and vibrant. In some cases, kinetics takes the form of a single element, such as the sliding doors that open near the top of the Twilight Zone Tower of Terror to reveal the rising and falling elevator cars, or the movement of the tea train as it climbs toward the Forbidden Mountain on Expedition Everest. In other cases, the Imagineers use "layers" of kinetics, such what you see as you move from Fantasyland toward Tomorrowland at Magic Kingdom, with the Astro Orbiter spinning alongside the PeopleMover in the foreground, while the Carousel of Progress building spins in the background. A common feature the Imagineers use to create kinetics are water fountains/features around the parks, such as the jumping fountains and reverse waterfall outside Journey into Imagination with Figment as well as the World Fellowship Fountain at Epcot.

Some other examples of kinetics found in the Disney parks are described in Alex Wright's *Imagineering Field Guides*:

- The Red Car Trolley at Disney California Adventure "adds an important kinetic element to the streetscape. Its movement activates the environment and augments the spatial relationships in the architecture".
- On Alice in Wonderland at Disneyland, "the loop exterior track … [is] a wonderful kinetic element that connects it to the relocated Mad Tea Party".
- Astro Orbitor at Disneyland serves as a "kinetic beacon into the world of Tomorrowland" while its counterpart Astro Orbiter at Magic Kingdom is "one of the primary contributors to the kinetics of Tomorrowland".
- Primeval Whirl and Triceratops Spin add kinetics to DinoLand U.S.A. at Animal Kingdom
- At the (now closed) Maelstrom attraction in the Norway Pavilion at Epcot, "the boat peeking out of the attraction provides movement in the courtyard".
- In Frontierland at Magic Kingdom, kinetics can be seen in the Splash Mountain runoff into the Rivers of America; rafts, the

Liberty Belle, and other watercraft moving around and near Tom Sawyer Island; and the passing riverboats, Walt Disney World railroad trains, and Big Thunder Mountain Railroad mine cars.

Kinetics are also often used in the design of wienies. A wienie at the end of an avenue that incorporates movement and kinetics is sure to grab the attention of approaching guests. We looked at examples of these "kinetic wienies" in chapter 10, including the Twilight Zone Tower of Terror, Expedition Everest, and Splash Mountain.

Alex Wright explains that another tool the Imagineers use to keep the Disney parks dynamic and active is what they refer to as BGM (background music), "the musical selections that fill in the audio landscape as you make your way around the park. Each BGM track is carefully selected, arranged, and recorded to enhance the story being told, or the area you have entered."

Beyond enhancing the kinetics of an area, background music can also serve different roles in different areas. In some areas, background music is inspired by and based on the music and songs from the area's attractions. For example, the background music in Cars Land at Disney California Adventure includes songs originally written for Mater's Junkyard Jamboree. In cases like this, the background music serves as a form of audio pre-show and post-show. Guests are first exposed to an attraction through the background music before experiencing the attraction, and then reminded of the attraction after they leave.

In other cases, an area's BGM is less specific, and intended to help enhance (and blend into) the setting. According to Alex Wright, the background music in Future World at Epcot, for instance, is "less about a specific time or place and more about a mood and the ideas being explored here. It's chosen by our media designers to reflect the soaring themes and concepts featured in Future World. It can't be pinned to a particular setting or genre, but completes the effect. You might not even notice that it's there as you make your away around, but you miss it if it's not."

In both examples, the BGM works in tandem with visual kinetic elements to create an active and dynamic environment. For instance, the examples of kinetics in Frontierland noted above also makes use of background music and other sound effects.

Background music can also help in transitions between areas, as

I noted in chapter 11, with the gradation of Main Street's upbeat music into the "growls and howls" of Adventureland, among other examples.

A Dynamic Experience

Kinetics is about *keeping the experience dynamic and active*. Anything you do to add movement or motion to your project (either literally or figuratively) can help keep it active and "moving".

Kinetics is especially useful when communicating ideas, such as projects that communicate or convey a message of some sort, or when promoting your projects and ideas. In both cases, kinetics can help keep your audience engaged. For instance, if you're creating a presentation, using animation (without over-doing it) and other different types of media (music, sound effects, etc.) can contribute to the kinetics of your presentation and help keep your audience's attention. Graphic design that employs active shapes can also contribute to the kinetics of a presentation or printed materials.

Another way to employ kinetics is through variety—distinguishing specific parts of the overall experience from one another. One way to do this is through using a variety of content and forms of content. Even something as simple as breaking up long blocks of text with bulleted lists or diagrams can help break up the reading experience and make it slightly more dynamic an experience than found when reading walls of words. A good example of employing variety is in instructional design, where we can create kinetic instructional experiences by combining different types of content, such as lectures, demonstrations, exercises, interactivity, and other activities.

The Pyramid in Practice—Kinetics

Because this book (like most) uses the written word, my options for kinetics are somewhat limited. I've tried to vary the text through different forms of content as well as different subject matter in each chapter. In addition, for those of you who have visited the Disney parks in the United States, I'm hoping to use your own memories to help provide some level of kinetics. The examples I've used are intended to invoke memories of the dynamic and active environments guests experience when visiting Disney theme parks.

Post-Show: Imagineering Checklist

Kinetics is *keeping the experience dynamic and active*. Variety is a simple and helpful way to employ kinetics.

- Is your project dynamic and active?
- How can you make your project more dynamic and active?
- How can you employ variety in your project?
- How can you add movement and motion to your project?

CHAPTER SEVENTEEN

The "it's a small world" Effect

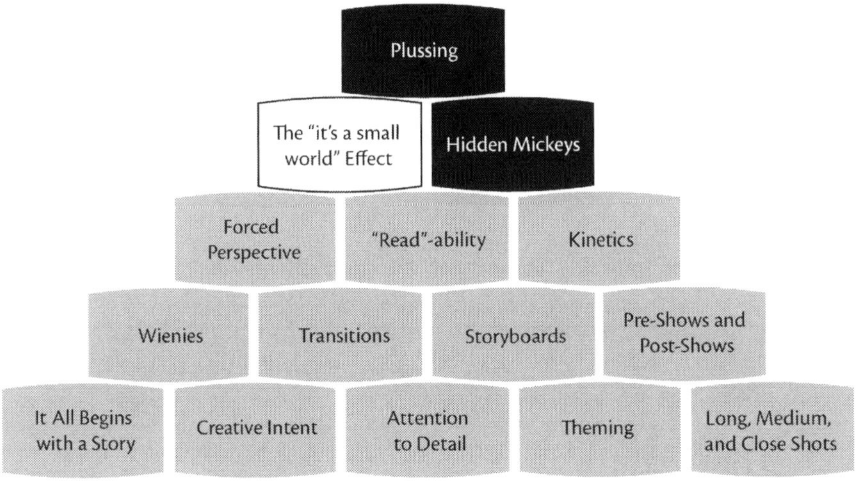

Plussing
The "it's a small world" Effect
Hidden Mickeys
Forced Perspective
"Read"-ability
Kinetics
Wienies
Transitions
Storyboards
Pre-Shows and Post-Shows
It All Begins with a Story
Creative Intent
Attention to Detail
Theming
Long, Medium, and Close Shots

Disney parks and attractions are designed to be memorable, and the blocks of the Imagineering Pyramid that form the Making it Memorable tier play a big part in that. These are practices focused on reinforcing ideas and engaging the audience. The first technique in this tier is what I call The "it's a small world" Effect. It's about using repetition and reinforcement to make an experience and message memorable. As its name implies, it's related to the so-called "Happiest Cruise That Ever Sailed", but as we'll see, there is more to it than that.

One of the primary ways the Imagineers employ repetition in the parks is through music. As Alex Wright explains, "Often the music or songs that serve as the soundtracks for our attractions are the most memorable part. The songs get stuck in your head and become a part of how our guests share their recollections of the Disney park experiences." If you've ever ridden on "it's a small world" at Disneyland or Magic Kingdom, you understand this principle. Typically, one visit is all it takes to get that song stuck in your head for a while, and it's likely that just reading the words "it's a small world" might start the song playing in your head. Note that I'm not suggesting that having that song in your head is a bad thing (though some might disagree). I quite like the song myself, but there's no denying that it stays with you.

But while it may be one of the more famous (or infamous) Disney theme park songs, "it's a small world" is hardly the only one that's memorable. In fact, there are a number of songs that are just as catchy and memorable, many of which were written by songwriters Richard and Robert Sherman. The Sherman brothers, or "the Boys", as Walt referred to them, wrote many of the most memorable songs in Disney's films and theme parks, and one of the keys to the Sherman Brothers' songs being so memorable is their use of repetition. Below are snippets from some of the most memorable theme park attraction songs written by the Sherman Brothers that illustrate their use of repetition.

One of the first songs they wrote for the Disney parks is the opening song in Walt Disney's Enchanted Tiki Room at Disneyland, "The Tiki Tiki Tiki Room":

> In the tiki tiki tiki tiki tiki room
> In the tiki tiki tiki tiki tiki room
> All the birds sing words and the flowers croon
> In the tiki tiki tiki tiki tiki room

These words form the chorus and are repeated no less than six times during the song.

For the 1964–65 New York World's Fair, the Sherman Brothers composed songs for two of the four attractions built by WED Enterprises. The first of these is "There's a Great Big Beautiful Tomorrow" from the Carousel of Progress:

> There's a great big beautiful tomorrow
> Shining at the end of everyday
> There's a great big beautiful tomorrow
> And tomorrow's just a dream away

> Man has a dream and that's the start
> He follows his dream with mind and heart
> And when it becomes a reality
> It's a dream come true for you and me
>
> So, there's a great big beautiful tomorrow
> Shining at the end of every day.
> There's a great big beautiful tomorrow
> Just a dream away!

The other song they wrote for the 1964–65 New York World's Fair is the one this technique is named for, "It's A Small World (After All)", that features this well-known stanza:

> It's a small world, after all
> It's a small world, after all
> It's a small world, after all
> It's a small, small world

Another favorite of mine is "One Little Spark" from the original Journey into Imagination at Epcot (also used in the current version of the attraction):

> Imagination, Imagination
> A dream can be a dream come true
> With just that spark
> From me and you

While the Sherman Brothers wrote more than their share of memorable songs for the Disney parks, they were not the only songwriters to employ repetition to craft memorable songs. Two classic attractions feature memorable and catchy songs that played a large part in their popularity and success. The first of these is "Yo Ho, Yo Ho, a Pirate's Life for Me" by X. Atencio and George Bruns from Pirates of the Caribbean, in which the title phrase "Yo Ho, Yo Ho, a Pirate's Life for Me" is repeated multiple times throughout the attraction. The other is "Grim Grinning Ghosts" by X. Atencio and Buddy Baker from the Haunted Mansion, where "grim grinning ghosts come out to socialize".

Like nearly everything in the Disney parks, the memorable nature of its songs is by design, and traces its roots back to Walt Disney. Arthur Levine, on About.com, writes: "According to [Marty] Sklar,

Walt Disney understood the importance of music in storytelling and placed a premium on it. When Sklar asked him once why he was spending so much time and energy perfecting a soundtrack for one of the attractions, Disney replied, "People don't go out of the park whistling the architecture."

Music is not the only way the Imagineers employ repetition to make the parks memorable. They also use repetition in other ways, such as through the use of pre-shows and post-shows in which key ideas and themes are presented both before and after an attraction (we looked at these in an earlier chapter). Repetition is also found in things as basic as park announcements. For example, one of the most well-known and oft-repeated phrases to guests at Walt Disney World can be heard when riding the monorail: "Please stand clear of the doors. Por favor manténganse alejado de las puertas." Monorail guests hear this phrase no fewer than 3–4 times during a trip around the Seven Seas Lagoon. For guests staying at a resort on the monorail such as the Contemporary, the Polynesian Village, or the Grand Floridian, this announcement will likely be playing in their heads long after they return home, just like "it's a small world after all".

In addition to repetition, the Imagineers use other tools to reinforce their story and creative intent, including many of the other tools in the Imagineering Pyramid that we've looked at in previous chapters, such as Attention to Detail, Theming, "Read"-ability, and others.

Repetition and Reinforcement

The "it's a small world" Effect is about *using repetition and reinforcement to make your audience's experience and your message memorable.* Employing this technique involves finding ways to reinforce key ideas and concepts, whether through simple repetition or by using multiple (and possibly different) means to communicate important ideas.

In the realm of training and teaching, concepts and skills are often reinforced by performing the same tasks or types of tasks multiple times. For example, schoolwork and homework don't typically involve students doing a particular type of problem only once. It's far more common for students to work on multiple examples of each type of problem, both in homework as well as on tests and exams. Likewise, effective training often has participants performing the same types of tasks multiple times. I recently got re-certified in CPR/First Aid and the use of AEDs (Automated External Defibrillators), and during that certification training, we had multiple opportunities to practice CPR skills and the use of the AED. As success coach Tony Robbins says, "Repetition is the mother of skill."

Repetition and reinforcement needn't take simple forms such as repeating lyrics or tasks. Some of the ideas we've already looked at in the Imagineering Pyramid can also be useful in reinforcing your message. For example, one approach to reinforcing might involve using "Read"-ability to present your ideas in a visual way in addition to using only words. This might be as simple as using graphic design or specific fonts, or as elaborate as a full-color illustration. Depending on the nature of your project, you can employ repetition through the use of graphic design or stylistic motifs. As noted above, pre-shows and post-shows relate directly to reinforcing ideas and concepts through repetition. In addition, if you also use appropriate theming (such as fonts, colors, and styles) in your "Read"-able concepts, pre-shows, and post-shows, your message will be even more effective. By way of a simple example, consider the difference between the following:

The Imagineering Pyramid
The *Imagineering* Pyramid

The use of the Walt Disney Script font in the second example helps reinforce the inspiration for the ideas and concept in the Imagineering Pyramid.

The Pyramid in Practice— The "it's a small world" Effect

The post-show sections at the end of each chapter are intended to help reinforce the ideas presented in that chapter. One of the other ways I've tried to reinforce the ideas in this book is through consistent repetition of the descriptions of each principle in the Imagineering Pyramid. My hope is that by consistently using the same phrases, readers will be more likely to remember them.

Post-Show: Imagineering Checklist

The "it's a small world" Effect is about *using repetition and reinforcement to make your audience's experience and your message memorable.* Beyond repetition, "Read"-ability, Pre-Shows/Post-Shows, Theming and other Imagineering techniques can help when reinforcing your ideas.

- Are you reinforcing key ideas and concepts?
- Are you using repetition to help reinforce ideas?
- How can you employ other Imagineering practices to help reinforce your ideas?

CHAPTER 18
Hidden Mickeys

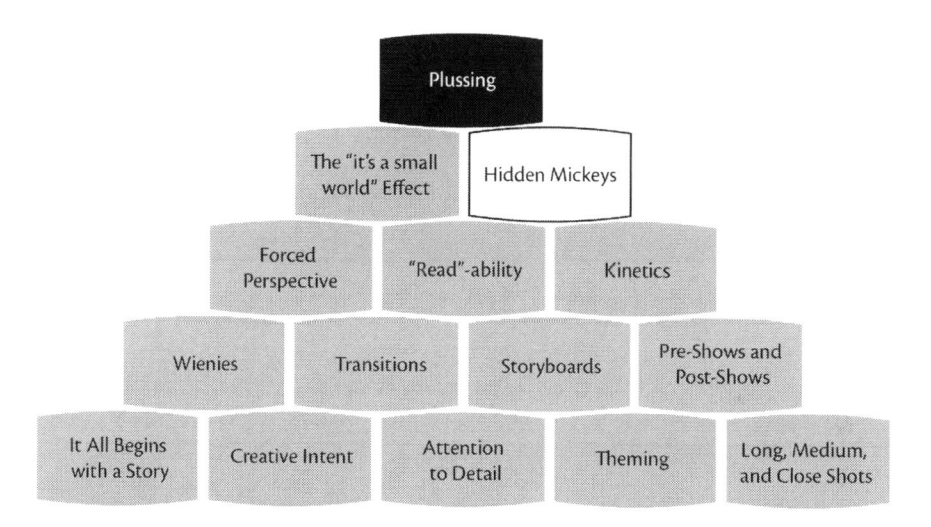

```
                    Plussing
          The "it's a small
            world" Effect      Hidden Mickeys
         Forced
       Perspective      "Read"-ability      Kinetics
                                                  Pre-Shows and
    Wienies        Transitions      Storyboards    Post-Shows
 It All Begins                      Attention                Long, Medium,
 with a Story    Creative Intent    to Detail     Theming    and Close Shots
```

The second (and final) block in the Making it Memorable tier is a technique the Imagineers use to engage their audience and have the audience take a more active part in the overall park experience: Hidden Mickeys.

According to *Hidden Mickeys: A Field Guide to Walt Disney World's Best Kept Secrets*, a Hidden Mickey is "a partial or complete image of Mickey Mouse that has been hidden by Disney's Imagineers and artists in the designs of Disney attractions, hotels, restaurants, and other areas. These images are designed to blend into their surroundings."

One of the bests way to understand Hidden Mickeys is to look at an example of one. The picture on the following page is from the queue at Expedition Everest at Animal Kingdom:

96   The Imagineering Pyramid

Copyright © Jeff Lange

Do you see the Hidden Mickey? If you look at the light switches near the patches, you can see that three of the light switches have been arranged in the shape of Mickey Mouse.

Copyright © Steven M. Barrett

One of the interesting things about Hidden Mickeys is that once you spot a Hidden Mickey, you never look at it the same way again. Once you see one of these, you never see what it really is, you tend to see the Mickey. For instance, I always see these light switches as Mickey Mouse first. Another interesting thing about Hidden Mickeys is that once you find a couple, you tend to want to look for more. Fortunately, there are guide books to help.

But, interesting as Hidden Mickeys might be to some Disney park fans, they aren't universally loved. Not even all Imagineers are fans of them. When asked about Hidden Mickeys in a project he worked on for a local hospital near Disney World, Imagineer Wyatt Winter replied:

> I'm not a huge fan of Hidden Mickeys. The reason for that ... we spend a lot of time trying to create these environments and stories and set you in a time and a place, and then it turns into "where's the Hidden Mickey?" Well, you're supposed to be riding through [an] 18th century haunted mansion in upstate New York, and now you're trying to find Mickey. So what's that balance? So we've done some other things where it's hidden references that fit in the story, so in Big Thunder, we put references to the original creator of Big Thunder or the original concept artist so it stays within that story a little bit, but it's not kind of a sore thumb.

These other references that Winter refers to are what are known as "Easter eggs", or sometimes "five-legged goats", named after the famous five-legged goat in Imagineer Mary Blair's mural in the Grand Canyon Concourse in the Contemporary Resort at Walt Disney World.

These are hidden tributes and secrets located through the Disney theme parks. Looking for five-legged goats and other hidden secrets within the parks is something that many Disney park fans enjoy. Like Hidden Mickeys, these hidden gems provide a way for guests to be more engaged and active during their visit. A few examples of other five-legged goats at the parks at Walt Disney World include:

- The listings on the train bulletin in the Main Street Train Station at Magic Kingdom include references to Disney Legend Ward Kimball ("Grizzly Flats" was the name of the private railroad he had in his backyard) as well as several old Disney movies, including *Pollyanna*.
- The names of several guides from early research trips to Africa during the design of Disney's Animal Kingdom park are commemorated on signs in the park.

- The props in Mickey's dressing room in Town Square Theater in Magic Kingdom include the sorcerer's hat from *Fantasia*, a crystal ball made by "Leota Crystals" (a reference to the seance room in the Haunted Mansion), and even a hand-drawn picture of Mickey Mouse and Oswald the Lucky Rabbit from a young fan of Mickey's named Jason (in reality, Imagineer Jason Grandt, who served as art director on Town Square Theater).

Involving and Engaging Your Audience

Hidden Mickeys are about *involving and engaging your audience* and providing ways for them to more actively participate in your experience. This active participation helps make the experience more memorable, and can greatly aid in learning. To quote Benjamin Franklin: "Tell me and I forget, teach me and I remember, involve me and I learn."

I'd like to engage you in an exercise that illustrates this idea, using an example from *In Pursuit of Elegance: Why the Best Ideas Have Something Missing* by Matthew May. Take a few moments to look at the following image:

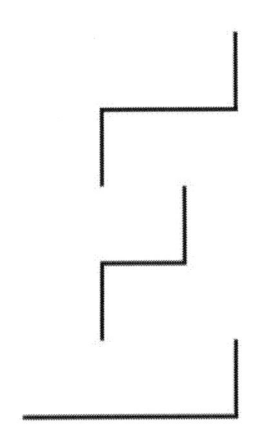

When you first look at it, what do you see?

It depicts something you use nearly every day. Can you identify it?

A key piece of information is missing, but once that information is shared, you'll likely never see the image in the same way again.

It's the upper-case version of the most common letter in the English language. The letter exists in the white space. (It's a capital letter "E".)

The first time I saw this I had no idea what it was, but since I learned to "see" what it really is, I never see anything else. What happens when your brain fills in the missing pieces in the image above is similar to the experience of finding a Hidden Mickey.

A similar technique is also used in the design of several famous and memorable logos such as the "arrow" hidden within the FedEx logo, and the "A-to-Z" arrow/smile in the Amazon logo. Finding ways to engage your audience like this isn't always easy, but it can be very effective at helping them remember you and your message.

Using Hidden Mickeys is about finding ways to involve your audience in the experience you want them to have. Making your audience active participants rather than passive observers will help engage them and make your project memorable. One way to engage your audience is to ask them questions. Whenever we're asked a question, our brains try to come up with an answer—we momentarily stop receiving input and respond—further involving us in the experience.

The Pyramid in Practice—Hidden Mickeys

I don't have any true Hidden Mickeys in this book, but I've tried to engage you by asking questions as part of the "Post-Show" section at the end of each chapter. The goal of these questions (and this book as a whole) is to encourage readers to consider how they can apply the principles of the Imagineering Pyramid to their own creative efforts.

Post-Show: Imagineering Checklist

Hidden Mickeys are *about involving and engaging your audience*. Asking questions is a simple way to engage your audience.

- How are you engaging and involving your audience?
- Are you providing ways for your audience to figure some things out on their own?
- Do you ask questions that force your audience to think about your message and how it applies to them?
- Have you incorporated the equivalent of Hidden Mickeys or five-legged goats in your project?

CHAPTER NINETEEN
Plussing

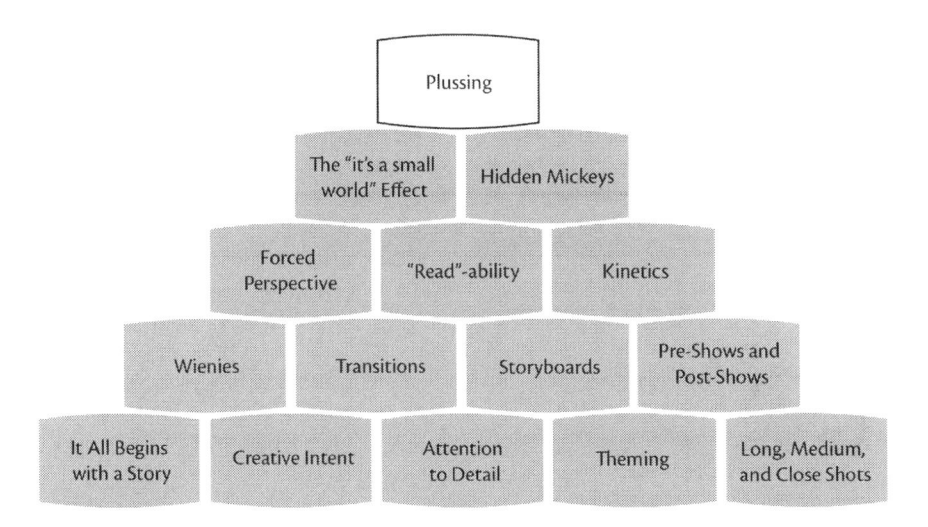

```
                    ┌──────────┐
                    │ Plussing │
                    └──────────┘
          ┌────────────────┐  ┌────────────────┐
          │ The "it's a small │  │ Hidden Mickeys │
          │   world" Effect   │  │                │
          └────────────────┘  └────────────────┘
    ┌──────────┐  ┌──────────┐  ┌──────────┐
    │  Forced  │  │ "Read"-  │  │ Kinetics │
    │Perspective│  │ ability  │  │          │
    └──────────┘  └──────────┘  └──────────┘
┌────────┐ ┌──────────┐ ┌──────────┐ ┌──────────┐
│ Wienies│ │Transitions│ │Storyboards│ │Pre-Shows and│
│        │ │          │ │          │ │ Post-Shows │
└────────┘ └──────────┘ └──────────┘ └──────────┘
┌────────┐┌────────┐┌────────┐┌────────┐┌──────────┐
│It All  ││Creative││Attention││Theming ││Long,Medium,│
│Begins  ││ Intent ││to Detail││        ││and Close  │
│with a  ││        ││         ││        ││  Shots   │
│Story   ││        ││         ││        ││          │
└────────┘└────────┘└────────┘└────────┘└──────────┘
```

Walt Disney was never one to rest on his laurels. He always wanted to do things better, and would constantly ask his people how they could "plus" things. Even when they thought something was already good, he would ask, "How could we plus it?" Plussing is the focus of the last block in the Imagineering Pyramid, which is also the only block in the top-most tier, and is what I call "Walt Disney's Cardinal Rule".

Alex Wright defines plussing as a "... term derived from Walt's penchant for always trying to make an idea better. Imagineers are continually trying to plus their work, even after it's 'finished.'" According to Pat Williams, in *How to Be Like Walt*, "Sometime during the 1940s, Walt [Disney] coined the term "plussing".... To 'plus' something is to improve it. Plussing means giving your customers more than they paid for, more than they expect, more than you have to give them."

Williams continues: "'Good enough' was never good enough for Walt Disney. He was a pioneer in plussing the art form of animated cartoons. He began by plussing Mickey Mouse with sound, then plussing the Silly Symphonies with color. Walt plussed the skills of his artists by sending them to art school at his own expense. Walt's relentless quest for excellence kept him at the leading edge of his industry—and left his competitors, well, nonplussed."

Walt Disney telling his workers to plus it, even when they thought they had done their best, gave Disney films an extra edge in quality animation. He employed this same philosophy in his live-action films, theme parks, and everything he did, and it has become a tradition within The Walt Disney Company, in general, and within Walt Disney Imagineering, in particular.

The Imagineers continuously focus on plussing in their design of the Disney parks, and look for opportunities to plus their work. According to Alex Wright, in *The Imagineering Field Guide to Disneyland*, "It's become our habit to rework the [Haunted Mansion] show when it comes back up from its annual 'Nightmare Before Christmas' overlay—mounted each fall by our partners at Disney Creative Entertainment—with new and surprising additions. Recent 'new magic' includes Madame Leota's head floating around the seance room in her crystal ball and a refined storyline told through a thoroughly reworked attic scene." As part of their on-going evaluation of the parks, the Imagineering Show Quality Standards team ask themselves how they might plus their attractions to best support their original creative intent. In some cases, this can be as basic and simple as a refurbishment in which the attraction is cleaned up, repainted, and polished, while in other cases it might mean a significant change in an attraction.

Some noteworthy examples of plussing include:

- *Star Tours: The Adventure Continues* Originally this attraction featured a single story, but now it features randomized story sequences including film footage from all of the *Star Wars* films. In addition, the quality of the video has been dramatically enhanced with the use of high definition 3D.
- *The Twilight Zone Tower of Terror* (at Hollywood Studios) The elevator drop was originally a simple pre-defined drop sequence which was the same every time, but it now features a randomized drop sequence so it's "never the same fear twice".

- *Test Track* In 2012, this attraction was significantly changed from its original concept of a General Motors testing plant to a Chevrolet Design Center where guests can design and test their own SIM Cars, with an entirely new design aesthetic.
- *Under the Sea ~ Journey of the Little Mermaid* A recent update to this relatively new attraction included new lighting and painting that brought a classic Disney dark ride feel to several key show scenes.
- *Haunted Mansion* (at Magic Kingdom): Updates to this classic attraction over the last several years have included new show scenes featuring Escher-like stairways, attic scenes featuring the Bride and her many deceased grooms, and interactive animated hitchhiking ghosts.

The Imagineers use plussing as a way to improve every element of the guests' experience. These can include updates and enhancements to not only the attractions themselves, but also attraction queues and surrounding areas. Examples of plussing to the queues of several attractions at both Disneyland and the Magic Kingdom include interactive elements to help engage the audience and keep them occupied while they wait in line (a very common complaint from guests is about the length of time they spend waiting). Adding interactive activities to queues helps distort the amount of time guests spend in line, and plusses the overall experience. Some of the attractions that include these updated queues include the Many Adventures of Winnie the Pooh, Haunted Mansion, Big Thunder Mountain Railroad, and (most recently) Peter Pan's Flight.

Plussing isn't limited to major attractions. Even some lesser-known areas of the parks are open to plussing as part of the Imagineers' efforts to continually improve the Disney parks. The Kidcot Fun Stops in World Showcase at Epcot are a good example of this. According to Alex Wright, in *The Imagineering Field Guide to Epcot at Walt Disney World*, Kidcot "...began life as little activity centers provided to give another level of activity for the kids who came to the park. The concept was plussed into something more connected to the countries of origin. The venues were developed into an appropriate look for each nation, with facilities designed to be kid-sized and fitted to each activity. The decor was chosen to reflect the nature of craft being performed."

"How Do I Make This Better?"

Plussing is *consistently asking, "How do I make this better?"* and constantly evaluating and revising your work based on feedback. This involves being deliberate about evaluating what you do, and looking for ways to improve it. The Imagineers use Show Quality Standards to ensure a consistent evaluation of what they do. Can you employ a similar approach in your work?

There's a reason why plussing is at the apex of the Imagineering Pyramid. Beyond the importance and value of consistent improvement, the placement of plussing illustrates that it is in fact supported and held up by the rest of the pyramid. Simply put, all of the tools in the Imagineering Pyramid can be used when plussing not only what you do, but also how you communicate and promote what you do. The summary descriptions of each of the principles in the pyramid can be turned into questions that can help when plussing your projects. Consider the following:

Are you...

... using your subject matter to inform all decisions about your project?

... staying focused on your objective?

... paying attention to every detail?

... using appropriate details to strengthen your story and support your creative intent?

... organizing your message to lead your audience from the general to the specific?

... attracting your audience's attention and capturing their interest?

... making changes as smooth and seamless as possible?

... focusing on the big picture?

... introducing and reinforcing your story to help your audience get and stay engaged?

... using the illusion of size to help communicate your message?

... simplifying complex subjects?

... keeping the experience dynamic and active?

... using repetition and reinforcement to make your audience's experience and your message memorable?

... involving and engaging your audience?

... consistently asking, "How do I make this better?"

One thing to note is that plussing doesn't always have to involve large-scale or sweeping change. Even small changes can make a big difference. In fact, a series of small incremental changes can often have a larger impact in the long run than a single major change.

My hope is that some of the ideas in this book inspire ways for you to plus what you do. Walt Disney believed in the power of plussing, and if there's one lesson to learn from Walt, let it be this one, in the words of Pat Williams: "Whether you are an NBA executive, a hotel maid, or a shoestring salesman, you can be like Walt. Pursue excellence in everything you do. Plus every experience—then plus the plus."

The Pyramid in Practice—Plussing

My attempts at plussing this book happen each time I sit down to write a section, whether it be continually searching for more and better examples of Imagineering principles, rewriting sections, or scrapping sections altogether.

Post-Show: Imagineering Checklist

Plussing is *consistently asking, "How do I make this better?"* The principles of the Imagineering Pyramid all relate to plussing. Small changes can make a BIG difference.

- How can you make your audience's experience better?
- Do you have your own version of WDI's Show Quality Standards?
- How can you apply other Imagineering Pyramid tools to your project to plus it?
- What little things can you add or change in your project that might improve the experience for your audience?

PART THREE
Imagineering Beyond the Berm

In Part Two we looked at the individual principles of the Imagineering Pyramid in terms of how they are used by the Imagineers in the Disney parks, as well as how each can be applied "beyond the berm". In Part Three, we're going to look at how the principles of the Imagineering Pyramid can be applied to some specific creative fields outside of Disney theme parks, including game design (chapter 20), instructional design (chapter 21), and management and leadership (chapter 22).

These fields are intended as further examples of how the Imagineering Pyramid can be applied "beyond the berm". Even if you don't currently work in any of these fields (in fact, I suspect that's the case for many of you), the examples of how the Imagineering Pyramid can be used in these fields will provide some insight into how they can also be applied to your own field, whatever it may be.

CHAPTER TWENTY
Imagineering Game Design

In this chapter we're going to look at how the principles and practices from the Imagineering Pyramid can be applied to game design. By "game design" I mean to include any of the varied tasks and activities involved in the design, development, and production of games. This includes game design and development, but also other areas as well, such as world building, graphic design, and interface design.

My own experience with game design is based on several years spent as a freelance game designer and in-house game designer and developer. My work was primarily focused on tabletop roleplaying games, but I also worked on a handful of board games and card games. Because so much of my experience is based on roleplaying games, many of the examples in this chapter will be based on roleplaying game design, but I've also included examples from other types of games as well. Roleplaying game design includes not only design of rules and game mechanics, but also world building and the design and development of supplemental material that helps gamemasters and players experience the game's setting.

While this chapter is about game design, this is not the place for extensive discussion of what is a game or the distinctions between games, puzzles, and toys. For those interested in learning more about these topics and about game design in general, I strongly recommend Jesse Schell's *The Art of Game Design: A Book of Lenses* (a second edition of this book was published in November 2014). Schell's book explores game design through the use of a series of principles and related "lenses", each of which offers questions that designers can use to evaluate their work. *The Art of Game Design* is full of excellent examples of game design principles in practice, and should be in the library of anyone interested in the field.

The Art of the Show

Knowing your mission, and ensuring that everything you do contributes to that mission

In the world of game design, your mission is to create games. Sounds simple enough, right? The truth is, your mission also has to account for the types of games you're designing. While games are most often used to entertain, they can also educate and inspire audiences. A recent trend in the field of instructional design is that of "gamification", which involves using "game thinking and game mechanics in non-game contexts to engage users in solving problems and increase users' contributions". A field related to gamification is that of so-called "serious games" in which games are designed for purposes primarily other than entertainment and can include educational games, but also games intended to increase awareness of social issues or simulate real-world issues. In her book *Reality is Broken: Why Games Make Us Better and How They Can Change the World*, Jane McGonigal argues that games offer solutions to help make the world a better place:

> What if we decided to use everything we know about game design to fix reality? What if we started to live our real lives like gamers, lead our real businesses and communities like game designers, and think about solving real-world problems like computer and video game theorists?

The game design "show" is not just about designing games, but also understanding the types of games you're designing and their goals. Are you designing fun or silly social games, serious war game simulations, or educational experiences that take the form of games? Whatever type you choose to design, that choice should serve as a lens through which you examine the decisions you need to make along the way.

It All Begins with a Story

Using your subject matter to inform all decisions about your project

What is your game about? That's the question at the heart of this principle. Everything about your game should relate to or support the subject matter of your game in some way.

Let's look at some examples of different types of games and the story or subject matter of each:

- *Earthdawn* is a tabletop roleplaying game about heroes building their legends as they try to reclaim their world in the aftermath of a magical apocalypse.
- *Magic: The Gathering* is a trading card game about "battle[s] between wizards known as "planeswalkers", who employ spells, artifacts, and creatures depicted on individual Magic cards to defeat their opponents".
- *Trivial Pursuit* is a board game about general knowledge and pop culture trivia.
- *Ticket to Ride* is "a cross-country train adventure in which players collect and play matching train cards to claim railway routes connecting cities throughout North America".
- *Super Mario Bros.* is a video game in which "the player controls Mario (in a two-player game, a second player controls Mario's brother, Luigi) as he travels through the Mushroom Kingdom in order to rescue Princess Peach from the antagonist Bowser".
- *Pac-Man* is an arcade video game in which the player controls Pac-Man and attempts to eat all of the pac-dots on a given level without being caught by one of his enemies (Binky, Pinky, Inky, and Clyde).
- *Temple Run* is an endless running game in which a character flees from demonic monkeys that are chasing him (or her).
- *Halo* is a series of "military science fiction first-person shooter video game[s] ... [about] an interstellar war between humanity and a theocratic alliance of aliens known as the Covenant".
- *Super Better, according to its creator,* is "a tool created by game designers and backed by science to help build personal resilience: the ability to stay strong, motivated and optimistic even in the face of difficult challenges".

The specific rules, mechanics, and other aspects of each of these games are based on and support its subject matter. For instance. the rules of *Earthdawn* encourage players to develop their characters' legends as they explore and travel the world left behind from the Scourge (the name for the magical apocalypse), "power pellets" in *Pac-Man* enable Pac-Man to eat his enemies, and the various obstacles in

Temple Run provide challenges as your character attempts to escape from the demonic monkeys.

Knowing your game's story is critical. During the entire design and development process, your game's story should be one of the primary sources of validation as you make decisions about the game. If an idea or element doesn't relate to or support your game's story in some way, it doesn't belong in your game. That's not to say it's a bad idea. It just doesn't belong in that particular game (but it might be the kernel of an entirely new game).

Creative Intent
Staying focused on your objective

In chapter 6, when we looked at Creative Intent, we noted that *a project's creative intent defines the experience the designer hopes to create for their audience*. At a fundamental level, the primary objective of a game should be the experience that people who play the game will have. In *The Art of Game Design*, Jesse Schell (a former Imagineer, interestingly enough) talks about the idea of experience when he says:

> What is the game designer's goal? At first, the answer seems obvious: a game designer's goal is to design games.
>
> But this is wrong.
>
> Ultimately, a game designer does not care about games. Games are merely a means to an end. On their own, games are just artifacts—clumps of cardboard, or bags of bits. Games are worthless without people to play them. Why is this? What magic happens when games are played?
>
> When people play games, they have an experience. It is this experience that the designer cares about. Without the experience, the game is worthless.

Later on in the same chapter, Schell reinforces this when he states: "The game is not the experience. The game enables the experience, but *it is not the experience.*"

Like your show and your story, your creative intent—the experience you want players to have when they play your game—should serve as a key criterion when deciding on elements to include in your game.

You might notice some parallels between "story" and "show". Similarly, just like a theme park attraction's story is often closely related to its creative intent (in fact, the two are very often inseparable), your game's subject matter (story) is directly tied to its objective (creative intent). These three principles (and others as well) are closely related, and you will rarely employ one without consideration of the others.

In game design, show, story, and creative intent form a sort of "continuum of narrowing focus" in which you zero in on the specifics of your game. Ask yourself the following questions as you design your game to help you along this continuum:

- What type of game am I designing? (**show**)
- What is my game about? (**story**)
- What is the experience I want players of my game to have? (**creative intent**)

Beyond the overall experience players of your game will have, there are also specific types of objectives to consider when designing a game. You may have specific design objectives, creative objectives, and even financial or business objectives. Most often these will also be tied to the overall experience, but are generally more limited and specific in scope. Let's look at some examples of games and game products that have specific types of objectives, including gameplay/mechanics objectives, and story/setting-based objectives.

Gameplay/Mechanics Objectives

Gameplay/mechanics objectives are focused on addressing needs specifically related to the game's mechanics and rules. Often, they're based on attempts to simplify the rules of the game to enhance the overall experience, but can also include attempts at creating innovative and creative approaches to solving problems. One of the best and most prolific game designers to do this is Jordan Weisman. Starting out as one of the founders of FASA Corporation (the creators of the *BattleTech* miniatures game, as well as the *Shadowrun* and *Earthdawn* roleplaying games), Jordan also founded Virtual World Entertainment LLC (creators of early location-based entertainment BattleTech Centers), Wiz Kids, LLC (creators of *Mage Knight*, *Hero Clix*, and other games), and most recently Harebrained Schemes (creators of *Shadowrun Returns* and *Golem Arcana*, among others). In addition, Jordan was involved in the development of some of the earliest alternate reality games (ARGs), including *The Beast* (developed to help promote the film *A.I.: Artificial Intelligence*) and *I Love*

Bees (developed to create "buzz" for the launch of *Halo*). Jordan has spent much of his career designing and developing games with specific creative objectives. A couple of the best examples of this are the *Mage Knight* and *Golem Arcana* miniatures games.

Mage Knight is a collectible miniatures game that combines roleplaying and wargaming elements. One of the design objectives of *Mage Knight* was to simplify the rules by moving as much information about the playing pieces onto the playing pieces themselves through "use of a dial wheel in the base of miniature figurines. The dial can be turned to reveal hidden information, representing the changing statistics of the figurine as the game progresses." As Weisman explains in a March 2003 interview on *Sequential Tart*:

> I was frustrated as a parent by the fact that miniatures games were either too complex or too expensive for most kids under the age of 16 to enjoy. So I set out to make a miniatures game that my sons and their friends would enjoy playing.... They don't want to spend a lot of time ... reading complicated rulebooks. They want to roll some dice, move some pieces around a table and have a good time. So that's what I wanted to give them with *Mage Knight*.

Golem Arcana takes this idea a step further, and moves the rules of the game into a mobile device. In an interview published on July 24, 2013, with IGN, Weisman describes *Golem Arcana* as "a tabletop game hybrid. It uses a smartphone or tablet to handle game rules and record keeping.... It takes what has traditionally been a genre of games that can be very intimidating, hard to learn, and sometimes hard to play, and makes them flow much faster."

The design of both of these games was strongly informed and influenced by the objective of streamlining gameplay by taking as much of the detailed record-keeping and rules out of the hands of the players as possible. For instance, the goal of moving game statistics about each figure to the figure's base meant that there would be a limit to how much information could be used. The physical limitations of the *Mage Knight* figures base determined how much information would be used to define the abilities of the individual figures.

Story/Setting-Based Objectives

Setting-based objectives are those focused on explaining, developing, or emphasizing some specific aspect of the game's setting or story. Many supplements and products developed for tabletop roleplaying games are based on these types of objectives. Two of the products FASA Corporation published for the *Earthdawn* roleplaying provide good examples of this type of objective.

One of the more unique aspects of *Earthdawn* is its treatment of magic, and in specific, its treatment of magical items. In many roleplaying games, if a character finds a magical item, they can often pick it up and start using its magic right away. In *Earthdawn*, before a character can make use of the magical properties of a magical item, he or she must first learn about the name and history of the item and then create a magical connection between it and themselves (via magical "threads"). Researching and learning the history of magic items can provide fodder for all sorts of stories and adventures, and we wanted to publish a supplement that was an example of how to incorporate magical items into a campaign. The product we ended up publishing was an adventure collection called *Blades*, which includes a set of adventures in which the player characters research and discover the history of a set of cursed magical daggers, the Blades of Cara Fahd. The objective of demonstrating how magical items work in the gameplayed a major part in how this book was designed, written, and developed. For example, the choice to use a set of magical daggers came from the need to provide a magical item that could be of use to multiple characters, unlike a single magical sword or suit of armor that would only benefit a single character. Also, the book needed to include a set of "interludes" between the adventures that served to link them together and provide the characters the information they needed to continue their research into the history of the blades.

Another product released for *Earthdawn* that served a specific setting-based objective was called *Prelude to War: An Earthdawn Epic* . Many of the games FASA Corporation published at that time, including *BattleTech* and *Shadowrun*, were set in "active" worlds, that is, worlds in which the setting changes as the timeline constantly moves forward. *Prelude to War* was designed to "activate" the *Earthdawn* game world and initiate an overarching story that would be told through subsequent products (a practice often referred to as "metaplot"). Up until we published *Prelude to War*, the *Earthdawn* setting was more or less static. With this product we introduced four significant events, the results of which would provide opportunities for the player characters to become involved in ongoing storylines that would be woven through future products.

The design of these products was strongly influenced by the setting-based objectives of each, whether discovering the secret history of the cursed daggers or initiating events that would forever change the *Earthdawn* game world.

Attention to Detail
Paying attention to every detail

Attention to Detail is important in any creative field, and game design is no exception. The details you use when explaining your game's rules or describing your game's setting can play a significant part in how the players will respond to your game. For example, in the context of roleplaying games, evocative details can help immerse your players into the setting of your game, while bland, unimaginative details can do your game and world a disservice.

You need to be careful when selecting the details you use, not only to ensure they convey the correct message, but also that they don't suggest or imply things about your game or game setting that you don't intend. I was guilty of this type of poor attention to detail when I worked on a supplement for the *Earthdawn* roleplaying game called the *Earthdawn Companion*. The *Earthdawn Companion* was intended to provide expanded rules for high-level play, but we also wanted to use it to help clarify some of the more unusual aspects of the game. As I noted above, the treatment of magic in *Earthdawn* is unique, not only in its treatment of magical items, but also in the way in which the magical patterns of characters can interact in the game. In *Earthdawn*, all places, objects, and living things with a proper name have a magical pattern, and characters can connect themselves to the magical patterns of others via objects known as pattern items. This can be a difficult concept to explain, so we provided a number of examples of pattern items and how they work in the game. In one, we used the example of a clove of garlic as a pattern item for a vampire. While the example worked to explain the relationship between the vampire and its pattern item, what I didn't consider at the time is that the example also established that vampires exist in the *Earthdawn* game world, something I had NOT intended or wanted. My lack of attention to detail resulted in my having to explain for years in online forums and message boards that vampires did *not* exist in *Earthdawn*.

In chapter 7, we talked about how *details draw attention to themselves*. This often manifests itself in published roleplaying game adventures in which descriptive text nearly always devotes more detail to items that the designer wants the player characters to notice and pay attention to. For example, when describing a room in a dungeon, if descriptive text provides little to no detail about three of the walls, but includes specifics about the fourth wall, that's typically an indication that the fourth wall holds something of interest to the player characters. What's interesting here is that detail need not always indicate danger or something of particular interest. Sometimes detail can be used as a red herring.

I was introduced to the idea of detail drawing attention to itself in the context of game design while at a seminar with game designer and author Tracy Hickman at the 1989 GenCon Game Fair. As part of a presentation about adventure/story writing, Hickman talked about this idea by citing an example of the classic *Advanced Dungeons & Dragons* adventure *Ravenloft* (written by Hickman and his wife, Laura). In the adventure, set in a "haunted" house that is home to the vampire Strahd von Zarovich, descriptive text includes lavish details about food spread out on a banquet table. As Hickman explained, this attention to detail led many, many players over the years to assume that the food was cursed or otherwise dangerous, even though that was not the case. *Ravenloft* uses the expectation that details will draw attention to themselves to keep players guessing what is and is not significant and help maintain the haunted house atmosphere of the adventure.

Theming

Using appropriate details to strengthen your story and support your creative intent

Theming can take different forms when applied to game design. In the realm of roleplaying game design and publishing, theming involves the use of appropriate and consistent graphic design, including fonts, colors, and even language. For instance, if you're publishing a game set in the distant future that features high levels of technology, you want to use a modern font (particularly for headings). An older or calligraphic font would clash (unless your game's setting made specific use of both modern and ancient styles). In terms of the language, the names you use for different elements of your game can help reinforce your story and subject matter. A good example of this is the game *Deadlands* published by Pinnacle Entertainment Group. *Deadlands* is set in the "Weird West", an alternate history that combines elements of Westerns, horror stories, and steampunk. To help reinforce this setting, several of the standard elements of rolelplaying games are given names that evoke the Weird West: dice are referred to as bones, the gamemaster is known as the Marshal, and the player group is called the Posse.

Other types of games can employ theming in different ways. When designing board games, the game board and other components such as the cards and tokens most often use graphic design elements that emphasize the subject matter of the game. For example, the graphic design of the board and cards in *Ticket to Ride* reflect the turn-of-the-century setting of the game, while the graphic design of *Magic: The Gathering* cards evokes its fantasy setting. In computer and video games, theming can be employed in the area of user interface design. Control panels and screens used to create and maintain characters should be designed in such a way as to emphasize the genre or setting. For example, the user interface design of *Skyrim* uses icons and symbols that evoke its setting, giving a very different look and feel from the user interface of a game set in a modern or future setting, such as *Halo*.

Theming can be even more elaborate depending on the nature of the game. Location-based games, for example, provide opportunities for extremely detailed and specific theming. A great example of this can be found at the *Pirates of the Caribbean: Battle for Buccaneer Gold* virtual reality game at DisneyQuest at Walt Disney World. In *The Art of Game Design*, Jesse Schell describes how the design team employed all manner of things to reinforce the theme of the game, including visuals, music, audio, the user interface (ship's wheels and cannons), and even the shape of the room in the which game is played.

Long, Medium, and Close Shots

Organizing your message to lead your audience from the general to the specific

When designing games, there are lots of situations in which you need to communicate information to your audience, and the use of long, medium, and close shots can be an especially effective tool for that.

An important place to use this technique is when explaining the rules and objectives of your game. For example, when writing the game's rules, you should start with a high-level overview of the object of the game and its victory conditions before providing details regarding movement, conflict resolution, or other specific game mechanics. A good example is often found in combat rules in roleplaying games, in which the rules provide an overview of the steps or phases of a combat round (determine initiative, resolve actions/attacks, determine damage, etc.) before providing the details of each.

Another use of this principle in roleplaying game design is in world building. When describing a fantasy setting, you can't start with close-up details. You need to introduce your world with establishing shots, explaining concepts in broad terms, and then follow up with more detail. This approach can be employed within a single product (in a chapter or section devoted to the game's setting) or across multiple products, each acting as a closer shot providing more details. For example, the *Earthdawn* core rulebook contains a chapter about Barsaive, the game's setting, that provides high-level descriptions of some of the main locations within Barsaive (long shot). One of the early supplements published for the game was the *Barsaive* campaign set that provided additional detail about many of the locales within Barsaive (medium shot). Later products such as *The Serpent River, Throal: The Dwarf Kingdom*, or *The Blood Wood* were focused on specific locations and provided extensive details about each (close shots).

In video games, long, medium, and close shots can be used in much the same way that they are in Disney theme parks and in films. Your establishing shot sets the stage for your game. As the player moves in closer to specific areas, more and more detail is revealed. A good example is the first view of Mean Street in *Epic Mickey*. The establishing shot of Mean Street helps communicate the idea that Wasteland is an alternate version of a Disney theme park. Starting with Town Square and ending at the hub, Mean Street conveys the atmosphere of Wasteland, with twisted buildings on either side of the street, and the looming and foreboding silhouette of the castle at the far end (a twisted counterpart to the charming and inviting nature of Main Street, U.S.A. in Disneyland). As players maneuver Mickey Mouse along Mean Street, additional detail comes into view, such as the shops themselves and opportunities for players to embark on small-scale quests.

Wienies
Attracting your audience's attention and capturing their interest

Using wienies in game design involves using whatever you can to capture your audience's attention and make them want to learn more about your game, including learning more about its setting or world or rules. Game design wienies can take several different forms, depending largely on the type of game, but also the objective of the wienie.

In video games in which players' characters can move about the game world, you can use wienies like the Imagineers use them in Disney theme parks, by creating interesting objects off in the distance that attract the player's attention, causing them to say to themselves, "I wonder what's over there?" These wienies—which are hopefully also "read"-able establishing shots—draw players into the game as they make their way toward the object of interest. The castle at the end of Mean Street in *Epic Mickey* works as a wienie leading the player down Mean Street and farther into the Wasteland, just like Cinderella Castle in Magic Kingdom draws guests down Main Street, U.S.A. and toward other areas of the park.

A similar effect can be used in roleplaying games by creating evocative and intriguing places within the game's setting that player characters will want to travel to and explore. For example, in *Earthdawn* there are several places whose names are intended to capture the attention of players and their characters, such as Parlainth the Forgotten City, the Badlands, Sky Point, and the Blood Wood. Note that most of these places are in fact quite dangerous, but for characters seeking to become legends and help heal the world, surely a little danger isn't going to slow them down.

Another form of wienie often used in game design is related to something game designer Greg Gorden calls the Nintendo Effect, in which a game's characters gain new abilities as they reach new levels. These new abilities serve as wienies enticing players to continue playing so their characters can "power up" and face even more obstacles and challenges. The Nintendo Effect is used commonly in video games (hence its name), but can also be used in roleplaying games, in which each level adds new abilities for players to choose from for their characters. These can take the form of spells ("Once

I get to 5th level, my wizard will be able to cast the *fireball* spell!"), magical items, special powers, and other abilities.

Lastly, as we discussed in chapter 10, creative chapter names can act as wienies in books, including roleplaying game rule books, adventures, and supplements, and encourage players and gamemasters to take the time to learn more about your game.

Transitions
Making changes as smooth and seamless as possible

You can use transitions in game design in a way similar to how the Imagineers use them in the Disney parks, to keep changes from distracting and disrupting your audience as they experience your game. Transitions can play a role in both play experience as well as in how you explain your game to your audience.

When writing the rules to your game, the order in which you present information can make a big difference in how quickly players are able to learn the game and its strategies. For example, if you're designing a card game, which do you describe first, the different types of cards used in the game or the rules for how the game is played? If you start with the types of cards, you run the risk of your audience getting lost in the details without understanding the context in which the cards are used. At the same time, if you start with the rules of gameplay, your audience might not grasp the subtleties of how different types of cards can impact play. One strategy to consider here is to use long, medium, and close shots, and start with a high-level overview of how the game is played and the types of cards as your establishing shot, and then explain things in more detail in later sections.

A similar question applies when writing and designing roleplaying game rulebooks. A long-standing debate in the roleplaying game design community is whether rulebooks should be written as reference guides, or as books to be read from cover to cover. Your decision will have a major impact on the order in which you organize the chapters of your rulebook. For example, do you include an in-depth step-by-step character creation process that players read through as they create characters, or do you include character creation details in individual chapters and have players reference the information as needed? Or, as above, do you strive for the best of both approaches?

Another use of transitions in roleplaying game design is in working out the order of encounters in game adventures. Many adventures tend to use easier, less dangerous encounters early on, saving the more dangerous, difficult ones for the end of the adventure, but mixing this up by including a difficult or dangerous encounter in the early part of an adventure could prove interesting (or troublesome!), so long as the encounter doesn't completely derail the story.

Gameplay transitions are also used in video games, including transitions that lead players between different parts of a single scene as well as between different scenes and types of scenes. In chapter 11, we looked at how transitions can be used within a game world (color transitions in *Epic Mickey*), but other games make use of similar techniques, such as changes in terrain and atmosphere. Transitions should also be carefully considered when leading players and your audience between cut scenes and game scenes. The unintentional use of a crash cut when transitioning from gameplay to a cut scene can distract players and take them out of your game experience. That said, if appropriate, the use of a drastic change can help communicate to players that something has changed. In either case, you should be deliberate about your choices regarding how you use transitions.

Storyboards
Focusing on the big picture

Storyboards are used in game design similarly to how they're used in Imagineering and other fields—to allow you to see the big picture and how the pieces of that picture can be organized. Some examples of how you can use storyboards in game design include:

- Planning sequences of scenes in a video game
- Designing the sequence of encounters in a roleplaying game adventure module
- Planning and organizing the rulebook for your game
- Grouping types of cards for a board game or card game
- Planning and organizing the contents of a roleplaying game rulebook or supplement
- Outlining potential sequences of activities possible in an alternate reality game or serious game

Pre-Shows and Post-Shows

Introducing and reinforcing your story to help your audience get and stay engaged

Pre-shows and post-shows are most often used in story-centric games (games in which the players participate in a story in some way), and not as often in board games or card games. Like in theme park attractions, they introduce your audience to your experience and reinforce the story or subject matter. While many card and board games can have story-centric elements, they tend to be more abstract than those used in roleplaying and video games.

Examples of how pre-shows and post-shows can be used in different types of games include:

- Introductory scenes in video games that provide background information and gameplay objectives
- Cut scenes before and after gameplay levels in video games that introduce and reinforce story elements and mission objectives
- Scenario descriptions that outline mission objectives in miniatures games
- Read-aloud text used to introduce encounters in roleplaying game adventures
- Short fiction used to introduce the characters and background in roleplaying game adventures and supplements
- Content provided for denouement or wrapping up loose ends at the ends of roleplaying game adventures

Forced Perspective

Using the illusion of size to help communicate your message

One primary use of forced perspective in game design is in the area of world building. In chapter 14, we looked at J.R.R. Tolkien's "distant mountains" as an example of forced perspective used in world building. You can use this same approach when creating and developing worlds for roleplaying and video games by using names and short descriptions of far-away places that make the world seem larger and more developed than it really is.

A good guideline when using forced perspective in this way is to provide as much detail as necessary, but as little as possible. You obviously want to provide enough information to give your audience at least a general idea of your far-away place, but you don't want to spend too much time on detail unless and until that place plays a larger role in the game. Keeping things vague and limiting the amount of detail you initially develop about your far-away places leaves you more freedom in developing those details if and when the time is right (for instance, if you are developing a specific product about that place). In fact, here's a little-known secret about roleplaying games. When you read about far-away places, or distant mountains, in roleplaying game books, odds are the designers haven't worked out all of the details about those places. They probably haven't even fleshed out much more than the short descriptions you're reading. At FASA Corporation, we did this sort of thing intentionally in all of our game lines, but let's look at an example from the setting chapter of the *Earthdawn* roleplaying game rulebook:

Iopos

Located in the northwest corner of Barsaive, the city of Iopos is ruled by a powerful family of magicians called the Denairastas, who have held power since before the Scourge. Though their success at bringing the city through the Scourge earned the Denairastas the loyalty of most of Iopos' population, the magicians continue to rule with an iron hand, arresting and often killing dissidents. The Denairastas subject outsiders to the same drastic measures as city residents, and so visitors to Iopos are advised to keep any comments about the city's rulers to themselves.

In the years since the opening of the kaers that followed the Scourge, the Denairastas have repeatedly vowed to defeat both Thera and Throal and claim control of Barsaive. Though the magicians currently lack the power to accomplish such a feat, they continue to gather magical and mundane forces.

The details provided here are sparse, but provide enough to give readers a vague idea of Iopos. In later supplements, we fleshed out more details about Iopos as needed, including specifics about the ruling family and other facets of the city. For instance, the Denairastas played a significant role in one of the events in *Prelude to War*, and at one point we decided that the secret of the Denairastas was that they were the progeny of a great dragon. We developed these details only when we needed to. Until Iopos started to play a larger role in the story of the *Earthdawn* game line, we intentionally left things vague and undefined and as one of our distant mountains.

"Read"-ability
Simplifying complex subjects

Games of all sorts often have complex rules or systems, and "Read"-ability is an ideal practice to help your players understand and learn how to play your game. One of the most basic ways in which you can use "Read"-ability in your games is through the use of illustrations and diagrams to help explain game mechanics and rules.

One common place where illustrations and diagrams are used in board games is in explaining the rules for how playing pieces can move around the board. For instance, some games allow pieces to be moved only in specific directions (forward only, forward or backward, left or right, etc.) while other games contain specific rules about whether a piece can move through a space occupied by another piece. Chess is a good example, where each type of piece has its own movement rules. In addition, some roleplaying games make use of a "grid" or map system in which character movement is tracked on specific spaces on the map. Roleplaying games of this type often have specific rules for how characters can move. Nearly all of these types of movement rules are more easily explained through "read"-able diagrams rather than via text. The old phrase "a picture is worth a thousand words" is very appropriate in situations like this.

Another common example of using "read"-able diagrams is found in rules for "scatter" in the combat rules of many roleplaying and war games. These rules are used to determine what happens when thrown weapons (such as knives or grenades) miss their target. In which direction did it miss? How far away from the target did it land? While not that important when throwing knives, when throwing an explosive this can have a big impact on the game, especially if an ally is near! Situations like this are most often resolved using a scatter diagram.

Diagrams aren't the only way to employ "Read"-ability in game rules. Examples and metaphors can also be effective ways of simplifying rules and systems when writing game rules. Examples can be used to illustrate both how specific rules work in the game, as well as how multiple aspects of the rules come together, such as in the case of gameplay examples that walk the reader through multiple turns with multiple players. In roleplaying games, metaphors are useful when explaining abstract concepts, such as how magic or other special abilities work. I noted earlier that one of the more complex ideas in the *Earthdawn* game is how characters interact via magical pattern items. In our attempts to explain this concept, we used different metaphors to explain the relationship between a character and their pattern items, as well as to explain how characters can use pattern items to interact with other characters.

In the design of video games, using "Read"-ability takes a slightly different form, in that in most cases players won't be reading the rules of your game, and will instead likely be learning as they play. In this case, the use of introductory "tutorial" levels that include instructions about specific aspects of gameplay can provide players the information they need to succeed in the game later on.

As you design the ways in which players will play your game, think about how you will explain it to them, and look for ways to simplify things. When looking for ways to simplify your message, consider the "six approaches to simplification" from *The Art of Explanation* (see "Simplification: The Heart of 'Read'-ability" in chapter 15).

"Read"-ability is especially important when it comes to mobile games, where the ability for players to quickly grasp how to play is key to a game's success. If players can't figure out how to play your game quickly and (relatively) easily, they will often drop it and look for another. In the case of mobile games, "Read"-ability isn't just about explaining the game, but is more about making the gameplay itself "read"-able. Consider the examples of a handful of extremely popular mobile games such as *Temple Run*, *Angry Birds*, and *Fruit Ninja*. Each of these features gameplay that is simple and very "read"-able, but still engaging enough to keep people playing (and playing and playing).

Kinetics

Keeping the experience dynamic and active

By their very nature, games are active and dynamic. The decisions and choices players make as they play games result in a different experience nearly every time (it's very rare when a game plays out in exactly the same way twice). That said, it's important when you design your game to include things that keep the gameplay experience dynamic and active for your players.

Designing active and dynamic gameplay can be as simple as incorporating different types of activities within your game. For example, including different types of levels and missions in video games can keep the experience more dynamic rather than have the player experience the same type of gameplay level after level. Employing even simple types of variety can help keep your gameplay experience more dynamic.

A simple example is the use of different perspectives in the *Halo* video game series, in which "players predominantly experience gameplay from a first-person perspective; the game perspective switches to third person when using certain weapons and vehicles".

A slightly more involved example of gameplay variety can be found in *Epic Mickey*, in which players encounter "transitional levels" interspersed throughout the game which provide a break in the game's story as well as variety in gameplay. Austin Grossman describes these transitional levels in *The Art of Epic Mickey*, noting that "[p]layers travel between different areas of Wasteland by jumping into movie screens and scrambling through a kind of cartoon subway system of obstacle courses. Each of these transitional areas takes a different classic Disney cartoon and turns it into a fast-paced game level where Mickey runs through a two-dimensional world of moving platforms, enemies, and barriers."

Other examples of variety in video games can be found in popular mobile games such as *Angry Birds* and *Candy Crush*, in which new special abilities and challenges are incorporated into each level.

Variety should also play a part in the design of tabletop games, including board games, card games, and roleplaying games. Variety in roleplaying games can come from the use of different mechanics for different types of abilities and actions. While the trend in roleplaying game design leans towards "unified" mechanics (in which a single mechanic is used to resolve all player character actions), I admit to having a soft spot for games that use different types of mechanics for different types of actions as they add a more dynamic feel to the game. For example, early editions of the *Dungeons & Dragons* tabletop roleplaying game used percentile dice roll to resolve the use of thief skills and other class-specific special abilities, but used a 20-sided die roll for combat actions. This difference keeps the gameplay experience more varied and dynamic. Something similar can be done in games that use a unified mechanic by offering different ways of interpreting results based on the type of action being performed.

A simple way to provide variety in board games and card games is to provide for different types of actions and strategies as part of the gameplay. Rather than having players all perform the same actions every turn, you can build variety and dynamics into your game by allowing players a choice between different types of actions each turn. The popular board game *Ticket to Ride* by Alan R. Moon uses this approach. Each turn, the player chooses one of three types of actions: draw train cards, claim a route, or draw destination cards. Each type of turn is useful at different points in the game, and keeps the game dynamic and active as each player makes different choices each turn as the game progresses. A similar kind of dynamic gameplay can be created in card games by allowing and encouraging players to combine different types of cards. *Magic: The Gathering* is a great example of this, and I believe one of the reasons for the game's popularity is the (seemingly) never-ending number of card combinations possible through skillful deck building and card play.

One last way to use kinetics in your game is to incorporate different types of physical activity and movement. A classic example is the board game *Twister*, in which you never know where you're going to have to put your arms and legs. Some card games involve the players moving the cards or their hands faster than the other players. A fun game of this sort is *Twitch: The Quick Reflex Card Game,* originally published by Wizards of the Coast (and sadly no longer in print), described as "... a race to run out of cards. So when a card says it's your turn, play a card and play it FAST". The cards fly fast and loose around the table in this game and players needs to stay on their toes to win.

The "it's a small world" Effect

Using repetition and reinforcement to make your audience's experience and your message memorable

The "it's a small world" Effect should be used to emphasize important concepts of your game. Victory conditions or specific restrictions are examples of things worth repeating or reiterating in your game's rules.

For instance, if there are specific restrictions on how playing pieces can be moved in a board game, repeating those restrictions can help ensure that players understand and don't violate them.

In video games, repetition can be used to help maintain a balance between the level of challenge your game presents to its players and the level of skill needed to play the game. Challenge and skill are both key aspects to consider when designing your game. In *The Art of Game Design*, Jesse Schell writes that "[e]very game requires players to exercise certain skills" and also notes: "Challenge is at the core of almost all gameplay. You could even say that a game is defined by its goals and challenges." These two concepts intersect in what Schell refers to as the "Lens of Flow", a concept related to what's known as the "flow channel". Based on research by psychologist Mihaly Csikszentmihalyi, we can think of "flow channel" in game terms as the balance between the challenges of the game and the skills needed to meet those challenges.

So, how does repetition factor here? A common pattern in video games involves a gradual and constant increase in the game's difficulty (challenges) as the player proceeds through the game. In order to keep players in the flow channel, it's important that we provide a means for the player to improve their skills in parallel with the increasing levels of difficulty. Employing repetition is one way to accomplish this. Requiring players to repeat specific moves over and over again as they progress through your game builds their skill level and allows you to increase the difficulty of the game without forcing the player out of the flow channel.

Hidden Mickeys
Involving and engaging your audience

As is the case with kinetics, by their very nature games involve and engage their audience. The mere act of playing a game involves and engages the players. But that doesn't mean that as game designers we can't do things to better engage our players, and using different types of Hidden Mickeys is one way to do so.

A simple example of Hidden Mickeys in game design can be found in the practice of including Easter eggs in video games. One of the earliest examples of video game Easter eggs is found in the 1979–80 Atari 2600 game *Adventure*. This game contains an "invisible" dot in one of the rooms of the black castle's catacombs. If this dot is carried to the east end of the yellow castle while other differently colored items are present, the wall flashes and allows the player to enter a secret room that displays the words "Created by Warren Robinett". Other examples of Easter eggs include hidden side quests, hidden weapons and tools, and graphics and images. Easter eggs can provide gameplay benefits such as new weapons or abilities, or hints to other games. Many players enjoy the hunt for Easter eggs, and they can provide a fun way for your players to engage with your game.

Another way to employ Hidden Mickeys in your game's design is by including "emergent gameplay", which "refers to complex situations in video games, board games, or table top role-playing games that emerge from the interaction of relatively simple game mechanics". Games in which a winning strategy is not obvious, and is learned and discovered through repeated play, often include emergent gameplay. Emergent gameplay allows players to discover new strategies and tactics by combining sets of simple rules and mechanics. Each new successful strategy found is akin to a Hidden Mickey in a Disney park, and like Hidden Mickeys, once a player uncovers an emergent strategy, the player's perception and experience of the game is forever altered.

Examples of emergent gameplay can be found in many types of tabletop games as well as trading card games like *Magic: The Gathering*. In trading card games, players combine different types of cards into their decks, and then play those cards in various combinations throughout the course of play. Players discover and create new strategies that emerge through repeated play with different card combinations. Emergent gameplay can also be found in role-playing games that feature a variety of character abilities that can be combined in new and interesting ways. In *Earthdawn*, for example, characters can combine various abilities (including talents, spells, and magical items) in different ways.

Plussing

Consistently asking "How Do I Make This Better?"

Plussing—constant improvement—should be a part of everything we do, and game design is no exception. As is the case in most fields, there are many approaches to plussing in game design.

A great source for ideas about plussing your game is Jesse Schell's *The Art of Game Design*. This book takes readers through the entire design process, and along the way presents a series of "lenses" through which you can focus on specific aspects of your design. Each lens provides a series of questions that can help you stay on track during the course of your design and plus your games.

One specific approach to improvement in game design featured prominently in Schell's book is that of "improvement through iteration" (Schell devotes an entire chapter of his book to it). One key part of this approach is what Schell refers to as the "Eight Filters". According to Schell: "Your finished design will eventually have to make it through eight tests, or filters. Only when it passes all of them is your game 'good enough'."

The eight filters and their associated questions are as follows:

1. **Artistic Impulse**
   Does this game feel right?

2. **Demographics**
   Will the intended audience like this game enough?

3. **Experience Design**
   Is this is a well-designed game?

4. **Innovation**
   Is this game novel enough?

5. **Business and Marketing**
   Will this game sell?

6. **Engineering**
   Is it technically possible to build this game?

7. **Social/Community**
   Does this game meet our social and community goals?

8. **Playtesting**
   Do the playtesters enjoy this game enough?

Another part of "improvement through iteration" directly related to Schell's eight filters is what he calls the "Rule of the Loop." Schell writes: "The process of game design and development is necessarily iterative, or looping. It is impossible to accurately plan how many loops it is really going to take before your game passes all eight filters and is 'good enough'." Put simply, the Rule of the Loop states: "The more times you test and improve your design, the better your game will be."

Another approach to improvement that should be part of any game design effort is playtesting. Like improvement through iteration, Schell devotes an entire chapter of *The Art of Game Design* to playtesting, which he defines as "getting people to play your game to see if it engenders the experience for which it was designed". The specific manner in which you playtest your game will vary depending on the type of game (for instance, you would playtest a board game differently than you would a card game or roleplaying game or video game), but every playtest should have a specific objective (or creative intent), and should be defined by the five questions that form Schell's "Lens of Playtesting":

> Playtesting is your chance to see your game in action. To ensure your playtests are as good as they can be, ask yourself these questions:

- *Why* are we doing a playtest?
- *Who* should be there?
- *Where* should we hold it?
- *What* will we look for?
- *How* will we get the information we need?

Lastly, another source for ideas for how to improve your game is the Imagineering Pyramid. Use the following questions to help you identify ways in which you can plus your game based on the other principles we've looked at in this book.

Imagineering Checklist Questions— Game Design

Principle/Practice	Questions
It All Begins with a Story	- What is your game about? - Have you evaluated the elements of your game to make sure they fit with your story? - How do you reinforce your game's story through your game rules?

Creative Intent	▪ What is your objective in designing your game? ▪ What is the experience you want players to have? ▪ Does your game have specific mechanics-based objectives? ▪ Does your game have a story or setting-based objective?
Attention to Detail	▪ Are you taking care to use appropriate details in your explanations and examples? ▪ How can you use specific types of details to influence your players as they play?
Theming	▪ Are you using graphic design elements that reinforce your game's subject matter or creative intent? ▪ How do the various elements of your game reinforce its story?
Long, Medium, and Close Shots	▪ Are you using establishing shots to present information to your players? ▪ How are you providing your players with more information about your game and its setting?
Wienies	▪ Are you using wienies to capture your player's attention? ▪ Can you use the Nintendo Effect?
Transitions	▪ How are you organizing the rules? ▪ Are the transitions between levels or areas of your game smooth or jagged?
Storyboards	▪ Are you using storyboards to plot out the story of your game? ▪ How could you employ mind-mapping or storyboard tools to help you organize your game rules or setting information?

Pre-Shows and Post-Shows	- Does your game use introductory scenes (or fiction) to help establish the setting? - Do you use cut scenes in your game? - How do you reinforce ideas to your players?
Forced Perspective	- How can you make your game seem smaller or simpler than it is? - Does your game world include distant mountains?
"Read"-ability	- Can you use illustrations to simplify certain rules and mechanics? - Could you use a metaphor or example to help explain abstract or difficult game concepts?
Kinetics	- How can you include dynamic and active gameplay elements? - Are you providing opportunities for interesting combinations of game elements? - Could you include physical activity?
The "it's a small world" Effect	- Does your game incorporate repetition to help players improve their skills? - Are you reinforcing the key concepts of your game enough?
Hidden Mickeys	- Does you game allow for players to devise their own strategies? - Does your game include Easter eggs that players can discover as they play? - Does your game include emergent gameplay?
Plussing	- Have you examined your game through the lens of Jesse Schell's eight filters? - How many times have you tested and iterated your design? - Have you playtested your game? Have you playtested it enough?

CHAPTER TWENTY-ONE
Imagineering Instructional Design

In this chapter we're going to look at how the tools from the Imagineering Pyramid can be applied to instructional design. In technical terms, according to M.D. Merrill, in a paper entitled "Reclaiming Instructional Design", instructional design is defined as the practice of creating "instructional experiences which make the acquisition of knowledge and skill more efficient, effective, and appealing". Put more simply, any time you design or create experiences with a goal of teaching something, you're engaging in instructional design. This can take different forms, such as the development of corporate training materials or presentations, or designing lessons for school classrooms.

As I mentioned in the preface, the concepts in this book first took the form of a presentation I gave at a learning/training conference about applying Disney theme park design principles to instructional design. While the connection between instructional design and Imagineering may seem odd at first glance (I can learn about teaching at Disneyland?), I believe the two are well aligned because *communicating ideas to an audience* is at the heart of both fields. In the case of Imagineering, it's about communicating a story to park guests, while in instructional design, it's about communicating new skills and knowledge to students.

The Art of the Show
Knowing your mission, and ensuring that everything you do contributes to that mission

In instructional design, your mission is to educate or train your audience in some way. The instructional design "show" is effectively communicating ideas to your audience. When developing instructional and/or training materials you need to remember that everything you do is about about creating an effective learning experience.

It All Begins With a Story
Using your subject matter to inform all decisions about your project

In instructional design, your story is the primary subject matter around which your learning experience is designed. Are you teaching about chemical reactions, the history of American theater, or how to install software on a computer? Whatever your subject matter, you should refer to it consistently when making decisions about your project. As you evaluate the pieces of your instructional design, you should ask yourself, "How does this support teaching about my subject matter?"

In addition to informing the topics and subject areas you want to cover in your educational experience, your "story" should also be used as a filter to determine what does and doesn't fit. In the midst of designing instructional materials, and in an effort to be comprehensive, it's tempting to include related topics that fall beyond the boundaries of your subject matter. We need to be careful when we're building instructional materials that we focus on our subject matter and limit the amount of extraneous or tangential topics.

Focusing on the story allows you to weed out tangential topics or subject matter that may not be appropriate. In chapter 5, I used the example of a first-aid training class and how that would not be the place to include information about different blood types. Another example comes from my experience designing functional and technical training for software applications. One of the courses I designed and delivered was based on an integration tool that employed different technologies to enable data transformation. While some of the training exercises for this integration tool employed some of those technologies, that course was not the place to explain them.

Creative Intent
Staying focused on your objective

In instructional design, your creative intent is the specific educational goal of the course—are you teaching functional knowledge, technical knowledge, some other kind of knowledge? Are you teaching someone how to answer customer support calls? Are you teaching chemistry or physics or history? Are you teaching somebody first aid? Are you teaching them how to implement a product? Your target audience should play a major role in determining the objective of your course. For example, an end-user training course has a different objective than an installation or implementation course. Everything you do should add something significant to the learning experience and should serve your creative intent.

Attention to Detail
Paying attention to every detail

Obviously, you need to use accurate and appropriate details to support your learning experience, because incorrect details can interfere with—and in some cases, obstruct—the learning. In addition, there's a balance to strike between not enough detail and too much. Finding that balance can often be challenging, but one approach to doing so is by asking yourself, "Does this support my subject matter and does it support my creative intent?" If you can't answer "yes" to both, you should reconsider including that detail.

Theming
Using appropriate details to strengthen your story and support your creative intent

In instructional design, theming is all about making sure your training delivers its message in a clear and consistent manner. Sometimes inconsistent theming can distract your audience, and you don't want to do anything that's going to take them out of the experience. Theming in instructional materials includes not just using appropriate words or images, but also includes consistent use of templates and styles and fonts and colors. Consistent theming fades into the background, while inconsistent theming can jar your audience and distract them from your content. In chapter 8, I described a training class I participated in where inconsistent use of fonts on a handful of slides drew my attention away from the subject matter.

Long, Medium, and Close Shots

Organizing your message to lead your audience from the general to the specific

In instructional design, using long, medium, and close shots means starting with general information before drilling down into more specific information. When you start a new lesson, you don't begin with details about some particular part of the subject matter—you want to start with an establishing shot before gradually pulling your audience into the details. For instance, in the case of product training, you might start with a high-level overview, and then move to a functional description, and then finally get to technical details about how and why a feature works the way it does.

An example of this principle can also be found in the basic process of developing an instructional design project. Every project starts with a high-level idea or concept such as, "Let's create a training course for our new software application." This is your long shot. As you develop that project, part of the development involves defining outlines and plans for the project such as, "This training course should cover installation, administration, and use of the application." These are your medium shots. Following this you'll likely drill down into greater levels of details, which comprise your close shots.

Wienies

Attracting your audience's attention and capturing their interest

In instructional design, using wienies involves highlighting specific objectives and/or exercises in a lesson, and outlining the overall learning objectives of the course. Instructional design wienies can also take the form of elements within your educational experience that draw your audience's attention and gets them to say things like, "I want to get to that lesson about 'XXX' that the instructor talked about in his course overview."

Transitions
Making changes as smooth and seamless as possible

In instructional design, transitions apply to the order and sequence in which we want to present our topics, and identifying the "best" order or sequence.

In some cases, the order in which you present information depends on basic prerequisites. For example, when teaching grammar, you wouldn't teach compound sentences before teaching simple sentences and the basic elements of grammar. One of the more fundamental aspects of designing learning or educational materials is identifying fundamental vs. advanced subject matter. Ironically, the better we understand something, the more difficult this can be.

As we become well-versed in our subject matter, we run the risk of falling victim to what authors Chip Heath and Dan Heath, in their book *Made to Stick*, call the Curse of Knowledge. "Once we know something, we find it hard to imagine what it was like not to know it. Our knowledge has 'cursed' us. And it becomes difficult for us to share our knowledge with others, because we can't readily re-create our listeners' state of mind."

In some situations, however, the order in which you present information is not so clear cut. I've found that training needs often call for presenting information in a different order than how things are done in the real world. For example, consider creating an exercise about a seven-step process for creating data in which step #3 includes four sub-steps (a, b, c, and d). In the real world, the process might be performed as steps "1, 2, 3a, 3b, 3c, 3d, 4, 5, 6, 7". However, in a training setting, you may want to present these steps differently to help your audience understand each step and sub-step of the process. For instance, you might focus on the main process and skip the sub steps (1, 2, 3, 4, 5, 6, 7), and then go back later in a separate exercise to cover the sub-steps (3a, 3b, 3c, 3d).

Storyboards
Focusing on the big picture

In chapter 12, we saw that storyboards can be used in instructional design to outline the entire classroom experience for a lesson, including lecture, quizzes, and exercises. In addition, you can use storyboards as a visual tool to allow you to "see" the entire course. Storyboarding can be done with a physical storyboard or with computer-based storyboarding or mind-mapping tools.

Pre-Shows and Post-Shows
Introducing and reinforcing your story to help your audience get and stay engaged

As noted in chapter 13, pre-shows and post-shows relate to a well-known saying often associated with public speaking, teaching, and training: "Tell your audience what you're going to tell them. Tell them. Tell them what you told them." In instructional design, you want to use pre-shows to identify the objectives and goals of a course or lesson, introduce topics, and make sure your learning objectives are clear to your audience. Likewise, you want to use post-shows to summarize key points in your lesson and and reinforce important concepts.

Forced Perspective
Using the illusion of size to help communicate your message

How does forced perspective apply to instructional design? Forced perspective means adjusting (or forcing, as the name implies) the perspective of your audience to help them understand something. One approach is to make topics/subjects seem smaller or simpler than they are. Even the most complex subject can be broken down into a small number of simple ideas, which can help prevent your audience from being overwhelmed when first learning large and/or complex subjects. Anything that helps communicate a complex subject in a simple way is related to forced perspective. This ties directly into our next idea…

"Read"-ability
Simplifying complex subjects

When designing an instructional experience, you want to use whatever devices you can to convey complex ideas in simpler terms. As we looked at in chapter 15, simplifying complex subjects can be accomplished by using a "big picture" overview, examples, illustrations ("a picture is worth a thousand words"), or metaphors. You can also look to the six approaches to simplification from *The Art of Explanation* for ideas to simplify your message (see "Simplification: The Heart of 'Read'-ability' in chapter 15). And while, unlike the Imagineers, you won't usually be constrained by time (you're not designing a dark ride, are you?), you still need to make sure the audience can quickly and easily understand your subject matter.

Kinetics
Keeping the experience dynamic and active

In instructional design, you want to keep your educational experience—whether it's a classroom lesson or a training session—dynamic and active by combining different types of content, such as lecture (but keep it lively!), demonstrations, exercises, and interactivity. If using presentations such as PowerPoint slides, you may want to use animation, as long as it's used sparingly and consistently.

Another approach to employing kinetics in instructional design is through the use of "gamification", or "the use of game thinking and game mechanics in non-game contexts to engage users in solving problems and increase users' contributions". The use of gamification in instructional design has become quite popular recently as more and more designers look for ways to involve and engage their audiences. Adding game-like activities to your educational experience is a great way to keep the experience more dynamic and active.

The "it's a small world" Effect
Using repetition and reinforcement to make your audience's experience and your message memorable

Repetition and reinforcement are intrinsically tied to instructional design. In *Wooden: A Lifetime of Observations and Reflections On and Off the Court*, legendary UCLA basketball coach John Wooden describes the importance of repetition and its role in learning:

> The four laws of learning are explanation, demonstration, imitation, and repetition. The goal is to create a correct habit that can be produced instinctively under great pressure.
>
> To make sure this goal was achieved, I created eight laws of learning, namely, explanation, demonstration, imitation, repetition, repetition, repetition, repetition, and repetition.

You should deliberately employ repetition and reinforcement in the design of any educational or instructional experience. This can be something as simple as repeating key concepts, either verbatim or in varying ways. Sometimes saying the same thing using different words helps people learn more effectively. Other forms of repetition might involve having students repeat a task or procedure. For example, if you're designing a training class for a financial application and several lessons relate to operations performed on or for a person's account, you may have your students create a new account for each exercise to help emphasize how accounts are set up in the application.

Hidden Mickeys
Involving and engaging your audience

Engaging your audience via Hidden Mickeys means providing ways for your students to come to learning on their own. When students discover some key piece of information on their own, or figure out how different pieces of something fit together, their view of that never changes and the lessons they learn tend to stick with them much longer. You can do this via questions that force students to think beyond the boundaries of your subject matter (such as questions that help students connect concepts learned in previous lessons to your current lesson), or you might use tests or quizzes that combine different concepts in slightly different ways.

One caveat here—you obviously don't want to deliberately leave important information out, but if you can structure your lessons so that the students put things together themselves, your lessons will be more memorable and have a bigger impact.

Plussing

Consistently asking, "How do I make this better?"

Constant improvement is something that makes sense in instructional design. You should constantly evaluate and revise what you do based on feedback, and ask yourself, "How can I make this better?"

The other principles of the Imagineering Pyramid are a great place to look for ways to improve what you do. The following questions will help you find ways to plus your educational experience.

Imagineering Checklist Questions— Instructional Design

Principle/ Practice	Questions
It All Begins with a Story	• Do you keep your subject matter in mind when developing your content? • Have you excluded tangential topics where appropriate and/or necessary?
Creative Intent	• Are you focusing on your target audience? • Do you evaluate how each element contributes to the overall goals of the course?
Attention to Detail	• Have you verified the details in your materials? • Are you including too much detail? Too little?

Theming	- Are you being consistent in your use of language and terminology? - Are you being consistent in your use of templates and formatting?
Long, Medium, and Close Shots	- Have you identified your establishing (long) and close shots? - Are you presenting information in a way that moves from the general to the specific? - Are you using different levels of detail to guide your audience through your material?
Wienies	- Do you provide compelling reasons for students to participate? - Have you explained what skills your audience can expect to learn?
Transitions	- Are you guiding your audience from subject to subject in a helpful manner? - How can you avoid being tripped up by the Curse of Knowledge? - Have you identified areas where you need to differ from "real world practice" in order to clearly communicate to your audience
Storyboards	- Have you outlined the entire classroom experience? - Have you stepped back to "see" the entire course? - Have you considered different ways to arrange the "events" of the course?
Pre-Shows and Post-Shows	- Do you outline your learning objectives? - Do you introduce your topics and how they relate to your subject matter and to other topics? - Do you reinforce your subject matter at the end of each lesson?

Forced Perspective	▪ Are you trying to adjust your audience's perspective to help them learn? ▪ Are you simplifying large or complex subjects?
"Read"-ability	▪ Do you use examples, illustrations, or metaphors to help explain complex subjects? ▪ Are you using the six approaches to simplification from *The Art of Explanation* to help simplify your message?
Kinetics	▪ Is your experience "active"? ▪ Do you use hands-on exercises? ▪ Have you developed demonstrations that illustrate the concepts addressed in your course? ▪ Does your course include quizzes, polling questions, or other interactive activities?
The "it's a small world" Effect	▪ Are you reinforcing key ideas and concepts? ▪ Are you using repetition to help reinforce ideas? ▪ Are you using repetition to help reinforce ideas?
Hidden Mickeys	▪ Are you providing ways for students to figure some things out on their own? ▪ Do you ask questions that force students to think beyond the boundaries of your subject matter?
Plussing	▪ How can you make your course better? ▪ What little things can you add or change in your course that might improve the learning experience for your audience?

CHAPTER TWENTY-TWO
Imagineering Management and Leadership

In previous chapters, we looked at the blocks of Imagineering Pyramid from the point of view of working on creative projects ourselves. From this point of view, we're the ones doing the bulk of the work on our projects, and we can apply the principles to our work and ourselves. But there is likely to come a time for many of us (perhaps all of us) when we move from doing the work ourselves to leading or managing others who are working on creative projects. The good new is that the practices and principles of the Imagineering Pyramid can also be useful when we find ourselves in a leadership or management role. When this happens, the nature of both our audience and the experience we hope to create changes. When in a management or leadership role, *your audience is the team of people you work with*, and *the experience you are creating is the experience your team has while working on your project.*

In this chapter, we're going to look at how the principles of the Imagineering Pyramid can be applied to management and leadership. I know some of you might be saying to yourselves, "I'm not involved in management or leadership." When we think of management and leadership we typically think of them in the context of business, but both apply outside of business as well. Like I used a broad view of game design in chapter 20, I'm taking a broad view of both management and leadership in this chapter. Any time you need to coordinate or lead the efforts of people to accomplish a specific creative project, goal, or objective, you're engaged in management and leadership. This can include something as simple as helping your children organize how they complete their homework and school assignments or as involved as leading a community volunteer project involving dozens or hundreds of participants.

Whether we realize it or not, most of us have been involved in some level of management or leadership at some point in our lives. Have you ever led a project team? Have you ever had to juggle multiple projects at once and organize your work so you can complete your projects on time? These are both examples of management and leadership. Beyond direct experience, those of us who have been in the professional working world for a number of years have all been exposed to different types of management and leadership in our careers, or have found ourselves in these roles in our personal lives.

In my career I've worked at many different levels of organizations, including those close to the bottom of the organization, as well as those in which I worked directly with presidents and CEOs. I currently work as a manager and leader with my current team. Outside of my work life, I've served as the chairperson on committees at my church as well as a leader for our local music booster organization. I think if you look at your own career and personal history, you're likely to find similar experiences of your own. Even if you aren't technically in a management or leadership role, I believe these principles can still help in whatever role you're in.

Before I go on, I ought to clarify something. Even though this chapter is focused on management and leadership, I don't mean to suggest that they are the same thing. They are far from it. In simple terms, leadership is about vision, while management is executing on a vision. In his bestselling book *The 7 Habits of Highly Effective People*, Steven R. Covey explores the differences between these two when he writes:

> Management is a bottom-line focus. How can I best accomplish certain things? Leadership deals with the top line. What are the things I want to accomplish? In the words of both Peter Drucker and Warren Bennis, "Management is doing things right; leadership is doing the right things." Management is efficiency in climbing the ladder of success; leadership determines whether the ladder is leaning against the right wall.

While management and leadership may not be not same the thing, they are closely related. Without a vision to execute against, managers would have nothing to do. As Covey writes in *Principle-Centered Leadership*, "Of course, management and leadership are not mutually exclusive; in fact, it might be said that leadership is the highest component of management." The bottom line is that leadership and management are separate but related, and the principles of the Imagineering Pyramid can apply to both.

Leadership vs Management: Walt and Roy Disney

The origins and history of The Walt Disney Company provide an excellent example of the relationship between leadership and management in the form of its founders, Walt and Roy Disney. In *Who's the Leader of the Club,* Jim Korkis writes: "Walt Disney was an inspirational leader ... and Roy Disney was an outstanding manager." He ends a short chapter called "Leaders and Managers: Walt and Roy" with this story: "Roy once told a group of reporters, 'My brother dreams of castles, but I am the one who has to actually build them.'" Without both Walt's vision and Roy's management expertise, the company we know as The Walt Disney Company might not even exist.

The Art of the Show

Knowing your mission, and ensuring that everything you do contributes to that mission

In chapter 4, we looked at the idea of your show being your mission, and how everything you do should contribute in some way to your mission. We also looked at some examples of businesses that struggled (and continue to struggle) because they lost sight of their mission. Being clear on the mission of the team you lead or manage is important, as is making sure you stay focused on that mission.

One way to stay focused is to develop and promote a mission statement. While most of us likely know what a mission statement is, let's look at a couple of definitions. In simple terms, a mission statement is a description of what an organization does, the business it's in, and and why it does it. A slightly more elaborate definition—this one from BusinessDictionary.com—defines mission statement as:

> A written declaration of an organization's core purpose and focus that normally remains unchanged over time. Properly crafted mission statements (1) serve as filters to separate what is important from what is not, (2) clearly state which markets will be served and how, and (3) communicate a sense of intended direction to the entire organization.

What I like about these definitions is that they both speak to more than just what the organization does. They also speak to the purpose of the organization and what's important to it. These points are at the heart of the value that mission statements provide. Like we talked about in chapter 4, your mission isn't just what you do—it's why you do it, and good mission statements should reflect that.

Good mission statements can also inspire and motivate not only leaders and managers, but individual contributors as well. For instance, when the people in your organization ask, "Why are we doing this?" a mission statement that speaks to helping customers rather than simply making money is more likely to help them stay on target. When decisions need to be made about next steps or how to proceed in a given situation, a strong mission statement can help keep you focused.

I'm a strong believer in mission statements at every level of an organization, because they help keep your people focused on the right thing and in the right direction. Just because your company has a mission statement doesn't mean you shouldn't also develop one for your department or team. Often, a corporate mission statement isn't applicable to the specific work done at the lower levels of an organization, and a team mission statement can help provide a more narrow focus for you and the people you work with.

It All Begins with a Story

Using your subject matter to inform all decisions about your project

When it comes to leadership and management, your story or subject matter comprises what you do (your job or function) and the specific subject, topic, or creative project on which you're working. When faced with making decisions on a project, ask yourself: "What is is our job?" and "What are the specifics of the project we are working on?"

What you do refers to the specific field in which you lead or manage people. For instance, if you manage a marketing team, you might make decisions related to a project differently than if you managed a quality assurance team or a team of technical writers or curriculum developers. The types of things you need to focus on when marketing a product are different than what you focus on when writing technical documentation for that product.

In addition to your specific field, domain, or job, your story also includes the specific topic of your project. For example, how you make decisions about a marketing plan will be different if you're marketing a product for a broad-based consumer market versus a product aimed at a technical market.

Creative Intent
Staying focused on your objective

In previous chapters we've looked at the importance of creative intent and staying focused on your objective when working on creative projects. When managing and leading creative people, your creative intent is the objective of a specific project, meeting, or activity.

One challenge facing many managers and leaders—and the people who work with them—is that we sometimes confuse our objectives and activities. The objective is what we want; the activity is what we do to get what we want. While in some cases the two might effectively be the same thing, they are distinct and separate. We often get so caught up in doing an activity that we lose sight of its original objective. We want to "check the box" even though, in some cases, we should have removed that item from our "to do" list altogether.

For instance, a common part of many product development processes is a series of review meetings at different stages in the development life cycle to make sure all the stakeholders agree on various aspects of the project, such as time line and specifications. The objective isn't just to meet; it's to make sure takeholders agree on important aspects of the project. A set of meetings is just one (and possibly the most efficient one) of the ways to accomplish that objective.

So, how can leaders and managers focus on their objective and creative intent, and make the distinction between objectives and activities? A good mantra for managers and leaders to adopt is:

What is our objective for this [meeting / project / effort / event]?

You should ask yourself this question consistently and about everything you do during your day. If you can't answer it, you should think about what you're doing and why you're doing it. Ask yourself, "Why are we doing this?" While similar to the first question, our brains look for different answers when we ask "why" questions as opposed to "what" questions (and the same goes for "who," "where," and "how" questions).

One answer that often comes up when asking this question is, "It's what we've always done." If you find yourself saying this, a little warning bell should be going off in your head, and it's time to look a little deeper to try to identify the original objective for this thing that you've "always done". This is a classic example of confusing your objective and the activities you perform to reach it. You shouldn't be doing that thing because you've always done it, but because it serves the original objective. The trick is to dig down through all the things you "always do" to find your objective.

One approach to this is to use a variation of the "5 Whys" problem-solving technique. Originally developed at Toyota Motor Corporation, "5 Whys" is "an iterative question-asking technique used to explore the cause-and-effect relationships underlying a particular problem. The primary goal of the technique is to determine the root cause of a defect or problem by repeating the question 'Why?' Each question forms the basis of the next question." When used in this context, instead of asking why something happened, you keep asking yourself why you're doing something until you arrive at the underlying objective.

Show, Story, and Creative Intent

As we saw in chapter 20, there are parallels between show, story, and creative intent. These three principles (and others as well) are closely related, and you will rarely employ one without consideration of the others. Show, story, and creative intent form a sort of "continuum of narrowing focus" in which you zero in on the specifics of your work. To navigate along this continuum, ask yourself:

- What is is our mission? What do we do? (**show**)
- What is our specific job in fulfilling our mission? (**story**)
- What are we working on now? (**creative intent**)

Attention to Detail

Paying attention to every detail

Attention to detail is important in every creative project, and is something that both individual contributors as well as leaders and managers need to focus on. As a leader, attention to detail can be a powerful tool in your management and leadership toolbox. Paying close attention to detail shows the people who work with you that you're engaged in their work and that you're committed to helping them succeed.

One of the challenges of taking on a management and leadership role is that as you lead larger groups of people it becomes more difficult to keep track of the details of the work those people do. In fact, at a certain point, it becomes nearly impossible for leaders and managers to know the details of every project. As Michael W. Preis notes in *101 Things I Learned in Business School*, "The higher one rises in an organization, the more one must be a generalist." But even if you find yourself in a more "generalist" role, it's important that you work on understanding the details related to the work your team does, and help the people who work with you to understand the details they need to know to do their jobs.

As a manager or leader, it will often fall to you to explain projects to your team, and that will almost invariably include drilling down into the details of a particular project. But as we saw in Chapter 7, introducing too much detail can overwhelm your audience, and the same is true here. You need to find the right balance between giving your team enough information to do their job without flooding them with so much detail they lose sight of the project's creative intent (making them lose sight of the forest for the trees, branches, and leaves).

A key part of paying close attention to detail for leaders is knowing when to share specific types of details with your team. Certain details typically apply to specific stages in a project. Some are important at the start of the project, while others only come into play at later stages of the project. The trick is to learn to identify what your team needs to know and when they need to know it. For example, if there are certain constraints related to the installation or construction of a large-scale project (such as the size of the space in which the project will be constructed or the amount of time that will be provided to install the project), those details need to be made clear at the start.

Finally, there is a risk we face when we focus closely on the details of the work done by people on our teams: that the work might not be done quite the way we might have done it (and hence, for many, it would be "wrong!"). As we look closer at what our people do, we run the risk of moving from paying attention to detail to micro-management. Despite similarities, there is a difference between the two.

In his article "Pay Attention to Detail and Innovate", Dr. Eric J. Romero explores the relationship between these two concepts, noting that micromanagement "is when a manager or leader assigns work, tells capable employees exactly how to do it, monitors them excessively, and often takes over when work is not done exactly as the manager wanted". In contrast, Romero says that "[p]aying attention to detail is what good managers and leaders must do to ensure that work is done properly and the organization's vision is advanced. It involves assigning work, allowing staff to do it their way, and making sure it gets done according to agreed standards."

Some key distinctions are in how the work is performed and the standards by which the work is measured. It's not (always) necessary that the people who work with you do things exactly how you tell them to do it, as long as they are getting the work done effectively and efficiently (even if your way is "better"). Likewise, when it comes time to evaluate the success of the work, it's not about making the manager or leader happy, but instead about meeting agreed-upon standards and criteria.

Theming

Using appropriate details to strengthen your story and support your creative intent

Theming is an important aspect of any creative project you manage or lead, but there is a specific aspect of it that's important when leading people: consistency. When choosing appropriate details with which to theme your project, you need to be consistent in terms of colors, textures, etc., to make sure your audience understands your message and isn't distracted by contradictions.

Likewise, when leading and managing creative people and creative projects, you need to be consistent in your message and your priorities. People look to their leaders for guidance when questions arise, and if you're not consistent when you communicate with your people, they can become confused and disengaged. This is not to say that change shouldn't or can't happen, but even if and when things change, you need to strive to be consistent in terms of your priorities and values.

Long, Medium, and Close Shots

Organizing your message to lead your audience from the general to the specific

Like many of the principles of the Imagineering Pyramid, the use of long, medium, and close shots is especially effective when communicating a message to your audience. Communicating high-level general information before providing details helps ease your audience into your message. In the case of leading and managing creative people and projects, your audience is your team, and this practice is helpful when you need to share information with them.

Two specific instances in which this practice is helpful are when you're first introducing them to a new project and when you need to introduce or communicate a change of some sort, either in the project or in your organization. When introducing a new project to your team, you want to start by outlining the big picture of the project and focus on what it is that you and your team will be developing. (This big picture, by the way, will also often reference your creative intent as well as your story.) Once everyone understands your establishing shot, you can then drill down into details about specific aspects of the project.

Likewise, when introducing a change of some sort, you should start with a summary of the change before focusing on how the change will impact the people on your team. For example, one type of change that many managers have to communicate with their people has to do with organizational changes such as management reorganization or layoffs. When sharing this sort of information, it's important to explain the reasons for the change before explaining that your team may have to work with different people in the future. See "Transitions", below, for more specifics about handling and communicating change.

Ironically, there are also times when you may need to invert this principle, and help the people who work with you move from the specific to the general, guiding them away from the details of their individual work to consider the overall project and the bigger picture. This happens when team members get so deep into the work they're doing that they lose sight of the project's objective and creative intent. For example, consider a team of Imagineers working in an attraction that involves some of the more technical Imagineering disciplines, such as ride system design, lighting design, or sound design. It's easy to imagine folks working in these disciplines getting so absorbed in the details of their work that they occasionally lose sight of the attraction's creative intent and story.

When this happens, it's the job of the leader to help the team members re-focus on their creative intent and step back to see the establishing shot. Neil Landau devotes one of his *101 Things I Learned in Film School* to this idea: "Make sure everyone is making the same movie.... Staff can't work at cross purposes, and must always understand the bigger picture into which their work fits. While interpretation is called for, it must be performed within the context of the larger vision."

One of the key jobs of any leader or manager is to help their team stay focused on the "big picture" (we'll look at this in more detail when we discuss storyboards later in this chapter) and long, medium, and close shots—as well as its inverse close, medium, and long shots—are good techniques for accomplishing it.

Wienies
Attracting your audience's attention and capturing their interest

Using wienies as a leader or manager is about capturing your team's attention and interest when presenting information about upcoming projects, objectives, milestones, or changes. This involves focusing your team's energy and effort on specific goals and objectives, and engaging them and getting them excited about upcoming projects, whether complete projects in and of themselves, or individual interim stages of a larger project.

Some specific things to focus on—specific wienies you can use—when introducing or presenting a new project to your team include the project's creative intent and story, your vision for the project, the need the project is intended to address, and how the project fits into the overall work plan for your team. We've talked about creative intent and story and their importance when working on creative projects several times, but haven't touched on vision or need much. This is because they are both more related to the overall creative process than the individual principles embodied in the Imagineering Pyramid.

We looked briefly at vision and the role it plays in Imagineering and creative projects in a previous chapter, but put simply, vision is a picture of what the project will look like when it's complete. As we noted in chapter 3, sharing your vision with the people you work with is important. Your project's need is the problem you're trying to solve ("We need to create a XXX").

Lastly, you need to outline how new projects fit in with other work your team is engaged with so they can better understand how these new projects will impact their jobs both in the short term and the long term. This is especially true if there is some form of overlap between existing and new projects.

In the case of large-scale and/or long-term projects, key milestones or deliverables within the overall project plan might be used as wienies as well. Important project milestones are like "sub-objectives" and can be promoted to your team as short-term targets for their focus. For instance, an important milestone in many construction projects is the date on which the final steel beam is installed in a structure. This milestone is often celebrated with a "topping off" ceremony in which members of the project team sign the final steel beam before it is hoisted into place. If a project you're working on includes significant milestones, you should consider using them as interim victories for your team to help keep them engaged through the life of the project.

Transitions

Making changes as smooth and seamless as possible

As a leader or manager, something that you will have to deal with at some point is change. Whether it's changes in personnel, changes in duties, or changes in objectives and goals, change of any type is nearly always disruptive, and part of your job as a manager or leader is to help guide your team through disruptions as smoothly as possible.

Though you may face many different types of change, at a fundamental level, there are two basic types you will encounter:

- Change that is *imposed on* you
- Change that is *initiated by* you

The nature of the change will impact how you address it with your team.

Changes imposed on you are typically those that originate from an external source, such as a customer or management, such as changes to your priorities and projects, changes in your budget or schedule, and changes in the size of your team resulting from reorganizations, resignations, lay offs, or terminations. The biggest challenge of changes imposed on you, regardless of where they originate, is that they are often unexpected and require that you quickly adjust to account for them.

Changes that you initiate tend to happen when you and your team identify better ways of doing your jobs (such as when you focus on plussing) or when you identify or create new projects to tackle. Change of this type will typically also involve coming up with plans and adjustments for how you will do things differently or take on your new projects. This will often allow you to be more proactive than reactive. One challenge with these types of changes is that you will likely need to sell or pitch your ideas to either your team or your own management and leadership (see "'Read'-ability" for more about pitching ideas).

Understanding the Change

Regardless of whether the change is imposed or initiated, you need to understand its scope and impact and how it will impact your team. One approach is to ask yourself and your team (and perhaps your management) a series of questions that help you better understand the extent of the change and how you can respond.

There are a minimum of three key things you need to know to fully understand the impact that a change will have on you and your team: the *what*, the *why*, and the *how*. These three identify *what* has really changed, *why* the change happened, and *how* you will accommodate the change.

Understanding the answers can help prepare you to address any type of change. The table below provides example what, why, and how questions for changes *imposed on* you, and changes *initiated by* you.

Change Imposed on You	Change Initiated by You
What has changed? • "Our deadline has been pushed up by 2 months." • "Our team has lost 2 members due to a reorganization."	**What is the change you want to propose?** • "We want to add a new offering to our selection of training courses." • "We would like to use different publishing tools to maintain our marketing website."
What is the reason for this change? • "Our customer has requested we deliver earlier than planned." • "Senior management has re-evaluated our priorities and another team needs some of our people."	**What is the reason for this change?** • "We need to remain innovative and competitive." • "Adopting a content management system to maintain our website will help us be more efficient and effective."
What do we need to do to accommodate this change? • "We need to dedicate more people to the project and consider authorizing overtime." • "We need to re-assign project work to the remaining members of our team, without overloading them."	**What do you propose you do to accommodate this change?** • "We'll re-assign some work to different people to free up a few team members to focus on this new offering." • "We need to send a few team members to training on the content management system, and brainstorm new ideas for how to best use it."

When answering questions about how to accommodate a change, look to some of the Imagineering foundations such as your show, your story, and your creative intent to help you develop plans to address the change that allow you to still focus on your mission, objective, and subject matter.

Communicating the Change

Once you understand the change and how it will impact you, you need to communicate your findings to your audience, whether by explaining an imposed change to your team or selling your management on an initiated change you want to make. Your goal is to communicate the change in such a way that it explains the nature of the change, but at the same time outlines how you and your team will accommodate it.

Exactly how you address changes of any type will be based on the specifics of your work, your team, and other factors, but you can use other principles from the Imagineering Pyramid when communicating changes. Some of the more useful principles include Long, Medium, and Close Shots (starting with an overview of the change before drilling down into the details of how that change impacts your team), Forced Perspective (making the change seem larger or smaller), and "Read"-ability (explaining the change and your plans to accommodate it in the simplest terms possible).

Storyboards

Focusing on the big picture

One theme we've touched on a number of times in this chapter is the idea that moving into a leadership or management role results in a need to focus on the big picture and to be more of a generalist. Storyboards are an ideal tool to help maintain this focus on the big picture.

You can use storyboards when doing strategic (and tactical) planning, outlining projects, developing or adjusting your processes (for example, in reaction to a change from your management) by putting key pieces of your process or project onto individual cards or sheets and arranging them so you can better understand how they all fit together. These storyboards can also be used to break up your "big picture" into smaller chunks that are easier to focus on.

You can also use storyboards to allocate your resources, including time, people, and money. For example, you can use colored index cards to indicate different resources and arrange and group them based on the different parts of your project to see if there is an imbalance of some sort ("We're going to only spend 2 months testing a new software module that took 7 months to build.") If you have different people from your team allocated to different aspects of a project, each might have their own card so you can see if you have too many people focused on one part of the project and not enough on another.

As we saw in chapter 12, there are other tools and approaches to storyboards that be useful here. Storyboards and mind mapping are helpful tools when brainstorming, as well as when reviewing the results of your brainstorming sessions in order to organize your ideas.

Pre-Shows and Post-Shows

Introducing and reinforcing your story to help your audience get and stay engaged

In Disney theme parks, audiences experience pre-shows and post-shows before and after an attraction. In the realm of leadership and management, these shows can be thought of as activities related to a specific project that you and your team engage in before and after you work on that project. More specifically, think of pre-shows as activities that prepare your team for an upcoming project, and post-shows as activities that follow the project and allow you to take stock of the work you've done and hopefully learn from the project. Perhaps the most common activities of these types are kick-off/introductory meetings and "lessons learned" or post-mortem meetings.

You should have a kick-off or introductory meeting every time you launch a new project, new process, or new strategy with your team. The goal of these meetings is to present the new "thing" (project, process, etc.) to your team so that they understand what it is they're going to be working on. Among the most important ideas to share in a kick-off of this type is the project's objective or creative intent and its subject matter or story (I told you these were important!), but you will also want to explain other information such as the project's milestones, the specific people who will be working on the project, and the impact (if any) that the new project will have on existing work. We talked about something similar earlier in this chapter when we looked at wienies, and the same points apply here, too.

As was the case with communicating change (see "Transitions", above), you can use other practices and principles from the Imagineering Pyramid when presenting new projects to your team. Storyboards can help you present the big picture (your establishing shot) and outline the various stages of the project; Long, Medium, and Close Shots provide a mechanism for introducing your new effort and leading your team from the project's general concepts down to the specifics; and "Read"-ability and Forced Perspective can help you simplify its more complex aspects.

Shortly after completing a project or launching a new initiative, postmortems or "lessons-learned" meetings provide a means to identify what went right, what went wrong, and how you and your team can improve in the future (in other words, how can you "plus" things). While a lessons-learned discussion can take many forms (an open discussion, a guided discussion, a brainstorming session), effective sessions include addressing the following questions (from "What is a Lessons-Learned Analysis", on ManagementIsAJourney.com), in order:

1. What did we expect to occur?
2. What actually happened?
3. What worked well, and why?
4. What did not work, and why?
5. What needs to be done differently?

It's important that you make it clear to your team that the goal of this meeting is improvement, and that any suggestions they offer will be taken under honest and serious consideration. Also, you need to make sure your team knows that they can be as honest as they can in these meetings, without any fear of reprisal or reprimand. Lessons-learned sessions are only valuable if everyone involved, starting with you, is committed to improving what you do and how you do it.

Forced Perspective

Using the illusion of size to help communicate your message

There will be times when leading people that it will be useful to make projects and challenges appear to be larger or smaller than they really are. Large-scale projects can be daunting to even the most prepared team, while small-scale projects are often dismissed as unimportant.

When first presenting a major new project or initiative to your team (either as part of a pre-show or a wienie), it can help to make it seem to be smaller than it really is so as not to discourage them before the actual work begins. In the case of projects or processes that involve a large number of steps or tasks, grouping (described in chapter 14) can help shrink the apparent size of the project when introducing it to your team. Likewise, for large and complex projects, consider using chunking (again, in chapter 14) to break it down into more manageable pieces. Obviously, at some point you need to share the actual scope of every project with your team, but when initially sharing information about upcoming work, using a little forced perspective can help get everyone on board.

At the other end of the spectrum, there will be times when you may want to make projects appear larger. For instance, when presenting results or requesting additional resources, sometimes it's necessary to present issues or challenges in a way that emphasizes their significance. For instance, if your team develops and updates documentation or training materials for periodic product releases, when presenting a summary of your team's work, citing the number of documents your team created might be more effective than simply listing the number of releases. Which seems more impressive: "We delivered 130 documents for 14 major releases this year" or "We updated documentation for 14 major releases this year".

"Read"-ability
Simplifying complex subjects

In your role as a leader or manager, there will be times when you need to simplify complex subjects to help communicate your ideas. Examples of this include some of the topics we've addressed in this chapter, including communicating change and presenting and pitching new ideas and projects to your team and to your upper management. In chapter 15, we looked at several different tools that can help when simplifying complex subjects, such as illustrations, examples, and metaphors. Here we're going to look at some specific examples of employing "Read"-ability when presenting and sharing information with the people you work with.

The first example is an executive summary. When providing a status update on a complicated project, look for ways to distill the details into a simple, "read"-able summary that senior managers and executives can quickly and easily understand. While you may have reams of details to share, senior leaders often don't have the time to sift through pages of detailed information, and need a summary of the big picture. As we saw when we looked at Attention to Detail, like you they've been forced to become generalists (probably even more so than you have!) and they rely on you and your team to focus on the details. Beyond reporting on a project's status, executive summaries can also be used to outline specific problems or challenges that may have arisen during the project that need immediate attention (and whenever you present a problem or challenge, you should make your best effort to also include a proposal for addressing that problem).

Another good example of "Read"-ability is the classic elevator pitch: a short, succinct spiel that explains new and/or complex ideas in simple, easy-to-remember terms. Elevator pitches are used often in traditional sales efforts, but are also useful when proposing new projects, ideas, and strategies.

Beyond the elevator pitch, there are other approaches to crafting an effective "read"-able pitch. In his book *To Sell Is Human*, Daniel Pink argues for other types of pitches, noting that "...today, when attention spans have dwindled (and all the people in the elevator are looking at their phones), [the elevator pitch] technique has become outdated". Pink's six "successors to the elevator pitch" include:

- **The One-Word Pitch**
  A pitch that distills your message to a single word.

- **The Question Pitch**
  A pitch that asks a question instead of making a statement.

- **The Rhyming Pitch**
  A pitch that—you guessed it—rhymes.

- **The Subject Line Pitch**
  Every email subject line is a pitch. Appeal to either utility or curiosity.

- **The Twitter Pitch**
  A pitch in the form of a tweet.

- **The Pixar Pitch**
  A pitch modeled on the narrative approach of a Pixar film ("Once upon a time there was _____. Every day, _____. One day _____. Because of that, _____. Because of that, _____. Until finally, _____.").

Kinetics

Keeping the experience dynamic and active

As we noted in chapter 16, one approach to creating an active and dynamic experience is through the use of variety. Just because many of the projects you and your team work on will likely involve the same types of tasks and activities, that doesn't mean you can't inject some level of variety into how you approach your work. Providing variety for your team can help prevent them from growing complacent or bored with doing the same things over and over.

One approach to variety is assigning your people to different types of projects and different types of work. If you tend to assign the same people on your team to a specific type of project, consider assigning them to other types of projects. This may require training some of them in new skills or how to use specific tools, but cross-training among the members of your team gives you more flexibility in terms of who you can assign to specific types of work. Now, there will be some instances where the skills and experience needed to do a specific job are unique enough that cross-training isn't really feasible. For instance, graphic design is a skill that usually takes a long time to develop, so it's not likely you'll be able to train copy writers to become graphic designers. But, if you have multiple graphic designers on your team who tend to focus on specific types of work, you might consider having those designers swap assignments from time to time.

Another approach to variety is to team up different sets of people from your team to work together on different projects. As new projects come up, think about members on your team that you could group together who haven't worked together before, or at least, haven't worked together recently. Asking your team members to work with different people can lead them to see things in different ways and from different perspectives, and new perspectives are very often the seeds of new ideas.

In the early days of WED Enterprises, Walt Disney teamed up different sets of people who had never worked together with great results. Rolly Crump had first-hand experience with Walt's approach to this when he was paired up with Yale Gracey to work on the Haunted Mansion. In *The Unauthorized Story of Walt Disney's Haunted Mansion*, Jeff Baham writes: "'Walt knew that I did little funky things, and Yale did little funky things, so he just put us together,' Crump said. 'I don't know how Walt picked him to come, but Walt was the best casting director that ever lived on the planet. So he decided that Yale and I should work together, but I didn't know Yale from up. I knew who he was, but that was about it.'"

An important facet to consider when assigning people to work together is understanding the strengths and weaknesses of the people who work with you. You don't want to create a group of people who all share the same strengths and weaknesses. Instead, you should look for ways to group people that have complementary skills and/or skills that offset each others' weaknesses. For instance, you wouldn't want to pair two people who both aren't especially strong with attention to detail, or who both tend to get so wrapped up in details that they lose sight of the bigger picture. A better approach would be to pair a big-picture person with someone who's better at focusing on details.

The "it's a small world" Effect

Using repetition and reinforcement to make your audience's experience and your message memorable

Repetition and reinforcement are useful tools when leading and managing people to ensure that your team understands the goals of the team and of the larger organization. If a goal or objective is important, it's worth mentioning more than once. If your team or organization has significant or important objectives (wienies), you can't tell them once and expect people to get behind them. You need to consistently remind everyone of the importance of any goal you plan to achieve with their help. Likewise, consistent repetition of your mission statement, core values, and vision can be an effective way of getting your people to embrace and support them.

Repetition is also a key ingredient when teaching and training your team members new skills and concepts. In the last chapter

I shared a quote from UCLA basketball coach John Wooden about the importance of repetition and its role as one of his "laws of learning". As Michael Preis notes in *101 Things I Learned in Business School*: "Repetition can be an effective way of learning: it drills information into our memories." You can't expect people to learn new things if they don't have a chance to practice, and repetition and practice go hand in hand.

Hidden Mickeys
Involving and engaging your audience

A sure-fire way to engage and involve your team is to help them to learn and grow and develop new skills and talents. Most people enjoy learning new things, so use that as a means to encourage your people to try new things. After all, you don't know what someone might be good at until you let them try. Challenge your people and push them to learn new things and discover and tap into hidden or latent talents that they might not even know they have. This requires that you get to know the people who work with you. Try to learn about their interests both on and off the job, and pay attention to the types of projects and tasks that they enjoy the most.

Part of what gave Walt Disney his reputation as—to use Rolly Crump's words—"the greatest casting director that ever lived" was his ability to identify and nurture hidden or under-utilized talents in the people around him. Two good examples of this are Imagineers X. Atencio and Blaine Gibson, both of whom ended up in roles at WED that were very different from where they started, thanks to Walt's insight.

X. Atencio had been an animator, but moved over to WED to work on the Primeval World Diorama before Walt assigned him to write the script for Pirates of the Caribbean. According to Jeff Kurtti, in *Walt Disney's Imagineering Legends*, Atencio recalled: "When I got over there [to WED], well, nobody knew what I was supposed to be doing. Then one day [Walt] called a said, 'I want you to do the script for Pirates of the Caribbean.' I had never done any scripting before, but Walt seemed to know that's what I could do." Atencio also wrote the script for the the Haunted Mansion and co-wrote "Yo Ho (A Pirate's Life for Me)" with George Bruns and "Grim Grinning Ghosts" with Buddy Baker.

Kurtti writes that Blaine Gibson was an assistant animator working with Frank Thomas when Walt learned that Gibson had been studying sculpture, so he put him to work sculpting figures for Disneyland, including "an Indian head for the Indian Village" as well as "Timothy Mouse for the top of Dumbo the Flying Elephant" and "the little devils for the hell scene of Mr. Toad's Wild Ride". When he was invited to join WED full time, Gibson was initially reluctant, but "[then] he was told that Walt had personally asked for him to move to WED. 'So, since Walt had that much faith in me to do something new, I went. I'll tell you, working at WED was a lot of fun.'"

Plussing
Consistently asking, "How do I make this better?"

Plussing has a long history and tradition within The Walt Disney Company, but it's not unique to them. The principles behind plussing are cornerstones in the teachings of some notable figures often associated with quality and constant improvement, including business consultant and father of the Total Quality Management approach W. Edwards Deming and former UCLA Basketball coach John Wooden.

In his book *Awaken the Giant Within*, success coach Anthony Robbins describes Deming and his influence on the Japanese business culture, noting that: "In 1950, [Dr. W. Edwards Deming] was brought to Japan by General MacArthur [and] began to train the Japanese in his total quality control principles.... Deming taught that quality was not just a matter of meeting a certain standard, but rather was a living, breathing process of never-ending improvement."

Writing about John Wooden's focus on continuous improvement, Blake and Mike DuBose write:

> Though now known for his outstanding record, Wooden spent 15 years at UCLA before achieving consistent winning streaks. He knew that the process would take time to perfect, and he encouraged smart risk-taking, saying, "Failure to act is often the biggest failure of all." By continually reviewing mistakes and successes while looking for opportunities to do better (a philosophy mirroring Deming's Total Quality Management principles), Wooden was able to perfect even the smallest details. He once said, "Success is never final; failure is never fatal. It's courage that counts"—a valuable message for personal and business life.

As these examples illustrate, the idea of constant improvement is not a new one in the world of management and leadership, whether in business or on the basketball court. No matter what sort of team you lead, always ask yourself and your team how you can improve on what you do. Using "lessons learned" sessions (see "Pre-Shows and Post-Shows", above) is one way to do this, but don't rely on that approach alone. Consistently asking simple questions like "How can we do XXX better?" and "How can we avoid making the same types of mistakes that often trip us up?" can help identify areas for focused improvement.

Lastly, as we've seen with game design and instructional design, the Imagineering Pyramid is a good source of ideas for improving what you do. Use the following questions to identify ways you can plus your work and team based on the other principles we've examined.

Imagineering Checklist Questions— Management and Leadership

Principle/ Practice	Questions
It All Begins with a Story	- What is your specific domain and how does it relate to your project? - What are some of the specifics of the project you're working on?
Creative Intent	- What is your objective? - What is the specific objective of your project or meeting or activity? - Is the objective still valid?
Attention to Detail	- Are you sharing appropriate details at the appropriate time? - What does the team need to know to complete each part of this project? - What does the team need to know to avoid challenges at later stages of the project?

Theming	- Are you consistent with your team?
Long, Medium, and Close Shots	- Do you use establishing shots to help introduce new ideas? - If you've been forced to become a generalist (through promotions/advancement) do you still take the time to focus on medium and close-up details with your team?
Wienies	- Do you share goals with your team in a way that helps inspire them? - Are you using milestones or key deliverables as wienies?
Transitions	- How are you managing change in your organization? - Do you really understand the change that is taking place (What, Why, and How)? - How can you most effectively communicate change to your team?
Storyboards	- Are you keeping the big picture in mind? - How do you communicate the bigger picture to your team?
Pre-Shows and Post-Shows	- Do you have project kick-off meetings? - Do you have lessons learned sessions after projects?
Forced Perspective	- How can you "shrink" the size of your project? - Are you promoting your team's efforts in the right way?
"Read"-ability	- Are you simplifying your message? - Are you using executive summaries or pitches when presenting your ideas?

Kinetics	- How can you assign different people to different tasks to keep your team active and engaged? - Are you looking for ways to assign different sets of people to work together? - Do you know the strengths and weaknesses of the people you work with?
The "it's a small world" Effect	- Are you employing repetition? - Are you employing repetition? - Are you consistently reminding your team about important goals and objectives? - Are you providing opportunities for your people to practice new skills?
Hidden Mickeys	- Do the members of your team have hidden talents that you can help them develop? - How can you learn more about your team members' interests both on and off the job?
Plussing	- Are you using "lessons learned" sessions to identify areas of improvement? - How can you and your team consistently focus on improvement?

Post-Show:
Final Thoughts and a Challenge

For my post-show, in this chapter I want to revisit the basic premise of this book, present you with a challenge, and offer some parting thoughts.

Creativity and the Imagineering Pyramid

"Creativity is not just for artists. It's for business people looking for a new way to close a sale; it's for engineers trying to solve a problem; it's for parents who want their children to see the world in more than one way." These words, taken from *The Creative Habit: Learn It and Use It for Life* by renowned choreographer Twyla Tharp, are at the heart of what this book is about. There is a creative aspect to nearly everything we do, and even the most seemingly mundane of activities can involve some level of creativity. I truly believe that. I hope you do as well.

In recent years creativity has become more and more valued, both in business and in other fields. Joshua Rothman, in *Creativity Creep*, writes: "[W]e're living through a creativity boom. Few qualities are more sought after, few skills more envied. Everyone wants to be more creative—how else, we think, can we become fully realized people?" A 2010 survey conducted by IBM's Institute for Business Values revealed that creativity is one of the traits CEOs value most among their employees, and is considered to be "the key to successful leadership in an increasingly complex world".

Along with this increased focus on creativity has come a seemingly endless stream of books, blogs, and other resources about that topic. As Rothman says, "Creativity is now a literary genre unto itself: every year, more and more creativity books promise to teach creativity to the uncreative." Most of these books and resources offer tips and techniques to help us "be more creative" or "generate new ideas" while others are more theoretical, exploring common traits of creative people and common misconceptions and myths about creativity. And while that's all well and good (I have a number of those books in my own library), I still think there is something missing.

What's missing is a model for the creative process—an example that we can look to for concepts and principles that can be applied across a variety of fields in the development and promotion of creative ideas. Where can we find a model like this? In a single word, Disneyland. Garner Holt, in his foreword to Jeff Barnes' *The Wisdom of Walt*, writes: "Disneyland is still the ultimate expression of the creative arts: it *is* film, it *is* theater, it *is* fine art, it *is* architecture, it *is* history, it *is* music. Disneyland offers to us professionally (and to everyone who seeks it) a primer in bold imagination in nearly every genre imaginable." More specifically, I believe the design and development of Disney parks, the practice known as Imagineering, provides an ideal model for developing and promoting creative ideas.

The Imagineering Pyramid

The Imagineers employ many different tools, techniques, and practices in their work. Of those, there is a set of principles—arranged in what I call the Imagineering Pyramid—that can serve as a model of the creative process for us in other fields that lie "beyond the berm".

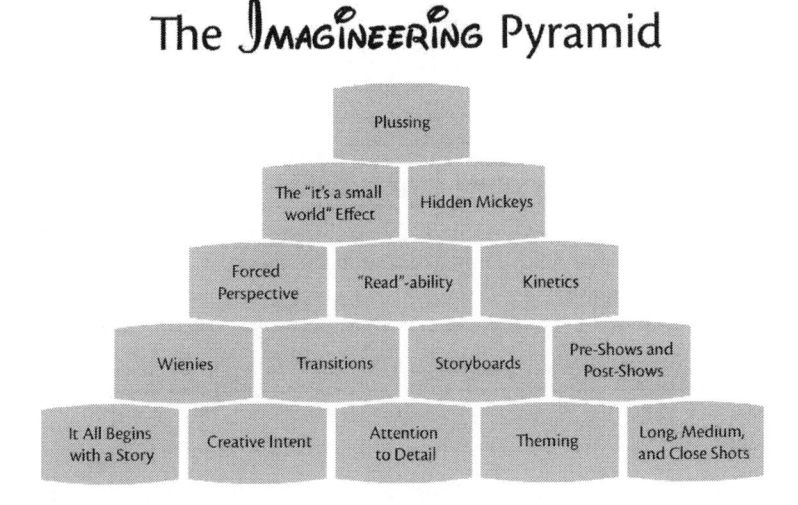

The Imagineering Pyramid

- Plussing
- The "it's a small world" Effect
- Hidden Mickeys
- Forced Perspective
- "Read"-ability
- Kinetics
- Wienies
- Transitions
- Storyboards
- Pre-Shows and Post-Shows
- It All Begins with a Story
- Creative Intent
- Attention to Detail
- Theming
- Long, Medium, and Close Shots

My goal with this book has been to describe the principles of the Imagineering Pyramid and how you can be use them to develop and promote your creative ideas. It's my hope that this book has caused you to think about how you can apply some of the Imagineering Pyramid principles to developing and promoting your own creative work. At a minimum I hope you use the questions from each chapter to evaluate your projects to look for ways to plus them. You can find a comprehensive list of these questions in "Appendix B: The Imagineering Pyramid Checklist".

A Challenge

I want you to use what you've read in this book and apply it to your own work. Think about a project you're currently working on (or will work on in the near future) and look for ways to apply the principles of the Imagineering Pyramid to that project. This can mean applying the pyramid to the project itself or to how you communicate and promote the project to others. For example:

Are you...

...using your subject matter to inform all decisions about your project? (It All Begins with a Story)

...staying focused on your objective? (Creative Intent)

...paying attention to every detail? (Attention to Detail)

...using appropriate details to strengthen your story and support your creative intent? (Theming)

...organizing your message to lead your audience from the general to the specific? (Long, Medium, and Close Shots)

...attracting your audience's attention and capturing their interest? (Wienies)

...making changes as smooth and seamless as possible? (Transitions)

...focusing on the big picture? (Storyboards)

...introducing and reinforcing your story to help your audience get and stay engaged? (Pre-Shows and Post-Shows)

...using the illusion of size to help communicate your message? (Forced Perspective)

...simplifying complex subjects? ("Read"-ability)

...keeping the experience dynamic and active? (Kinetics)

...,.using repetition and reinforcement to make your audience's experience and your message memorable? (The "it's a small world" Effect)
...involving and engaging your audience? (Hidden Mickeys)
...consistently asking, "How do I make this better?" (Plussing)

But My Project Is Different

One thing you will find as you start to apply the Imagineering Pyramid to your projects is that the manner in which you leverage and apply these principles will vary with different types of projects. For example, you probably noticed that the principles manifest differently when applied to game design, instructional design, and management/leadership. That's not a just a happy accident. It's also possible—perhaps even likely—that one or more of the principles won't apply to every single creative idea you pursue. The truth is that not every tool is suited to every job. This is so even in the case of Disney park attractions. Not every attraction makes use of every principle in the Imagineering Pyramid. You may recall that even among the Imagineers there are differences of opinion about some of these principles and how they are used in the design of Disney parks and attractions, such as Marc Davis' views on "storytelling" and Wyatt Winter's views on Hidden Mickeys.

If you find that one or more of the principles don't apply to one of your projects, PLEASE don't discard the rest of the pyramid. Instead, take the time to consider how you might apply as many of the principles to your work as you can. You might be surprised at just how flexible and versatile the Imagineering Pyramid can be.

Thank You

Thank you for taking the time to read this book. Time is the one resource that we can't get more of, and I appreciate you deciding to spend some of your time with me to learn about Imagineering and the Imagineering Pyramid. As I said in the preface, I'm still on my "journey into Imagineering" and this book has been the latest step for me on that journey. Writing it forced me to look even deeper at the Imagineering Pyramid principles and has served to reinforce my passiona s a student of Imagineering. Now it's time for my next lessons.

Thank you for joining me on this part of my journey. I'm glad you came along.

APPENDIX A
My Imagineering Library

This appendix includes lists of the books, videos, and other resources in my Imagineering library.

Books

A Brush with Disney: An Artist's Journey, Told Through the Words and Works of Herbert Dickens Ryman, David Mumford and Bruce Gordon.

Building a Better Mouse: The Story of the Electronic Engineers Who Designed Epcot, Steve Alcorn and David Green

Designing Disney: Imagineering and the Art of the Show, John Hench (with Peggy Van Pelt)

Designing Disney's Theme Parks: The Architecture of Reassurance, Karal Ann Marling (editor)

Disneyland Paris: From Sketch to Reality, Alain Littaye and Didier Ghez

Dream It! Do It!: My Half-Century Creating Disney's Magic Kingdoms, Marty Sklar

Expedition Everest: Legend of the Forbidden Mountain—The Journey Begins

HATCH!: Brainstorming Secrets of a Theme Park Designer, C. McNair Wilson

It's Kind Of A Cute Story, Rolly Crump

Marc Davis: Walt Disney's Renaissance Man

One Little Spark!: Mickey's Ten Commandments and The Road to Imagineering, Marty Sklar

Pirates of the Caribbean: From the Magic Kingdom to the Movies, Jason Surrell

Poster Art of the Disney Parks, Daniel Handke and Vanessa Hunt

The Art of Walt Disney World Resort, Jeff Kurtti

The Disneyland Story: The Unofficial Guide to the Evolution of Walt Disney's Dream, Sam Gennawey

The Disney Mountains: Imagineering at Its Peak, Jason Surrell

The Haunted Mansion: From the Magic Kingdom to the Movies, Jason Surrell

The Haunted Mansion: Imagineering a Disney Classic, Jason Surrell

The Imagineering Field Guide to Disney California Adventure at Disneyland Resort, Alex Wright

The Imagineering Field Guide to Disneyland, Alex Wright

The Imagineering Field Guide to Disney's Animal Kingdom at Walt Disney World, Alex Wright

The Imagineering Field Guide to Disney's Hollywood Studios at Walt Disney World, Alex Wright

The Imagineering Field Guide to Epcot at Walt Disney World, Alex Wright

The Imagineering Field Guide to the Magic Kingdom at Walt Disney World, Alex Wright

The Imagineering Way: Ideas to Ignite Your Creativity, The Disney Imagineers

The Imagineering Workout: Exercises to Shape Your Creative Muscles, The Disney Imagineers

The Making Of Disney's Animal Kingdom Theme Park, Melody Malmberg

Theme Park Design: Behind the Scenes with an Engineer, Steve Alcorn

Walt Disney Imagineering: A Behind the Dreams Look At Making the Magic Real, The Imagineers

Walt Disney Imagineering: A Behind the Dreams Look at Making MORE Magic Real, The Imagineers

Walt Disney's Epcot Center: Creating the New World of Tomorrow, Richard R. Beard

Walt Disney's First Lady of Imagineering, Harriet Burns, Pam Burns-Clair and Don Peri

Walt Disney's Legends of Imagineering and the Genesis of the Disney Theme Park, Jeff Kurtti

Periodicals

"Disneyland Is Good for You" (from *New West Magazine*, December 1978), Charlie Hass

This interview with Imagineer John Hench is one of the earliest analyses of Disneyland and how the Imagineers create the "magical" experiences that guests enjoy when they visit Disney theme parks, and should be considered must reading for anyone interested in learning about Imagineering. It is also one of the first articles (if not THE first) to describe the idea of "reassurance" as one of the key hallmarks of Disney theme park design. In his foreword to *Designing Disney:*

Imagineering and The Art of the Show, Marty Sklar describes this interview as "the single clearest analysis of Walt Disney's Magic Kingdom ever printed, before this book". http://scribd.com/doc/17664805/Disneyland-Is-Good-For-You.

The "E" Ticket Magazine

The "E" Ticket, devoted to "collecting theme park memories", was named after the coveted "E ticket" at Disneyland that admitted the bearer to the most popular rides and attractions. The magazine "was started by brothers Leon and Jack Janzen in 1986. The fanzine's intent was to not only provide a detailed history of the brothers' favorite park, but also give readers knowledge about the artists, Imagineers, and other creative individuals responsible for the magic of Disneyland."

In December 2009, Jack Janzen sold all of the assets of *The "E" Ticket* to the Walt Disney Family Museum. Several back issues, including three CD-ROM collections, are available from the museum's retail store. *The "E" Ticket* is a fantastic resource for those interested in Imagineering and Disney theme park history. For more information about *The "E" Ticket*, visit http://waltdisney.org/blog/e-ticket-magazine.

Audio Books

More Cute Stories, Vol. 1: Disneyland History, Rolly Crump

More Cute Stories, Vol. 2: Animators and Imagineers, Rolly Crump

More Cute Stories, Vol. 3: Museum of the Weird, Rolly Crump

More Cute Stories, Vol. 4: 1964/65 New York World's Fair, Rolly Crump

More Cute Stories, Vol. 5: Animators and Imagineers Part 2, Rolly Crump

More Cute Stories is a series of audio books recorded by Rolly Crump that are essentially appendices to his book *It's Kind of a Cute Story*. These feature short and often funny stories about the people Rolly worked with during his time at The Walt Disney Company.

DVDs

Disneyland Resort: Imagineering the Magic

Magic Kingdom: Imagineering the Magic

The Science of Disney Imagineering: Design and Models
Walt Disney Treasures—Disneyland—Secrets, Stories & Magic
Walt Disney Treasures—Tomorrowland: Disney in Space and Beyond

Online and Other Resources

NASA Information Technology Summit Day 2—Walt Disney Imagineering—Jack Blitch

In 2010, NASA held its first information technology summit, and the speakers included Jack Blitch, Vice President of Walt Disney Imagineering in Orlando. During his talk, Blitch describes the process Walt Disney Imagineering uses when they design and build attractions, with a specific emphasis on their use of technology and modeling software. Video of the summit is available online at the C-Span website: http://c-span.org/video/?295077-1/nasa-information-technology-summit-day-2. The portion of the video featuring Jack Blitch starts at the 50:00 minute mark.

Creative Mornings—Walt Disney Imagineering: Jason Surrell, Alex Wright, & Jason Grandt
Creative Mornings—Wyatt Winter: Walt Disney Imagineering

Creative Mornings is a breakfast lecture series for the creative community held in various cities around the world. These two lectures in Orlando feature Imagineers from the Orlando branch of WDI. Video of the lectures are available online at http://creativemornings.com.

Dining with an Imagineer (Hollywood Brown Derby—Disney's Hollywood Studios)

This is a dining experience available at Walt Disney World in which a small group of guests have lunch with an Imagineer (I described my family's lunch with an Imagineer in the preface). Learn more at http://disneyworld.disney.go.com/dining/hollywood-studios/dine-with-an-imagineer.

The Imagineering Model: Applying Disney Theme Park Design Principles to Instructional Design

As I mentioned in the preface, the Imagineering Pyramid began as part of a presentation I gave at a learning and training conference in 2011 which I later updated for a webinar I presented in 2013. The *Imagineering Model* also includes a simplified version of the process the Imagineers use when designing and building attractions. I originally planned to include the Imagineering Process in this book, but in the end decided to leave it out for various reasons. I will be writing a follow-up book focused solely on the Imagineering Process at some point in the future. Both versions of the *Imagineering Model* presentation are available online at Scribd.com and SlideShare.net.

Imagineering Field Guide Indices

As part of my research for this book (and my on-going interest in Imagineering), I created indices for all six of the Imagineering Field Guides, noting every reference to Imagineering terms and concepts, attraction names, Imagineers, and illustrations. These proved quite helpful when I was looking for examples of specific Imagineering principles while writing this book. I also combined the indices into a single master index of all the Imagineering Field Guides.

- Imagineering Field Guide Master Index
- Imagineering Field Guide to Disney California Adventure Index
- Imagineering Field Guide to Disneyland Index
- Imagineering Field Guide to Disney's Animal Kingdom Index
- Imagineering Field Guide to Disney's Hollywood Studios Index
- Imagineering Field Guide to Epcot Index
- Imagineering Field Guide to Magic Kingdom Index

You can find them on Scribd.com as well as in this public Dropbox folder: http://tinyurl.com/IFG-Indexes

Recommendations for Learning about Imagineering

As you might expect, I can recommend all of the books, magazines, DVDs, and videos listed above, and if you're a Disney park fan, I expect you may already own some (or all) of them. However, for those of you newer to Imagineering, the list might seem daunting. With that in mind, here are a handful of specific recommendations for anyone interested in learning more about Imagineering.

Walt Disney Imagineering: A Behind the Dreams Look At Making the Magic Real

This beautiful coffee table book is one of the first published about Imagineering (originally released in 1996). It provides an excellent overview of Imagineering and the Imagineering process, and includes LOTS of amazing concept artwork.

Designing Disney: Imagineering and the Art of the Show

This book by John Hench is, in the words of Imagineer Alex Wright on Twitter: "the closest thing we have to an Imagineering textbook". It explores the art and craft off Imagineering like few others, and should be in the library of anyone interested in understanding Imagineering and themed entertainment. Hench's book was a major resource for me when writing this book and during my research into Imagineering.

Imagineering Field Guides

Another primary source for this book were the Imagineering Field Guides by Imagineer Alex Wright. These small pocket guides provide concrete examples of Imagineering principles in practice. Don't be fooled by their small and simple appearance; they contain a wealth of information about Imagineering, as well as lots of excellent photos and art work.

Walt Disney's Imagineering Legends and the Genesis of the Disney Theme Park

One of the best ways to study a subject is to learn about the people involved in it, and Jeff Kurtti's book is a great way to learn about Imagineering by learning about the earliest Imagineers. The book contains profiles of the first generation of Imagineers, starting with Walt Disney and the people he brought into WED Enterprises when planning and designing Disneyland, and ending with John Hench ("the Renaissance Imagineer"). This book reinforces the idea that Imagineering was born from people from different disciplines adapting the skills and techniques from their disciplines to craft the new art form of theme park design.

One Little Spark: Mickey's Ten Commandments and the Road to Imagineering

Published in September 2015, this book by Imagineering executive Marty Sklar is one of the more recent addition to my library. It explores "Mickey's Ten Commandments", which Sklar created "to explain to and remind Imagineers about the foundation principles on which our success has been built". This book also includes examples of how the Imagineers have both succeeded and failed at each of the ten commandments over the years, as well as a series of short essays by current (and former) Imagineers about how they joined Walt Disney Imagineering.

To Learn More...

If you're interested in learning more about the resources in my Imagineering library, including links to online resources and videos, visit "My Imagineering Library" board on Pinterest:

https://www.pinterest.com/louprosperi/my-Imagineering-library

APPENDIX B
The Imagineering Pyramid Checklist

Most of the chapters in this book have included questions to help you apply the concepts and principles from the Imagineering Pyramid to your own projects. This appendix collects all of those questions in a single Imagineering Pyramid checklist that you can use to evaluate and "plus" your projects.

The Imagineering Pyramid

- Plussing
- The "it's a small world" Effect
- Hidden Mickeys
- Forced Perspective
- "Read"-ability
- Kinetics
- Wienies
- Transitions
- Storyboards
- Pre-Shows and Post-Shows
- It All Begins with a Story
- Creative Intent
- Attention to Detail
- Theming
- Long, Medium, and Close Shots

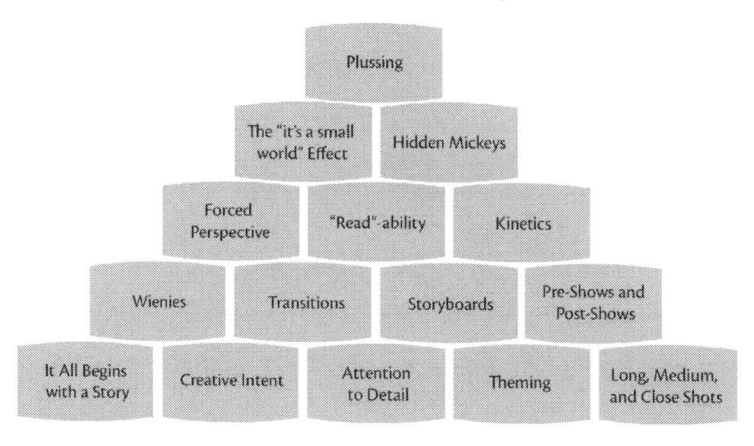

The Art of the Show

Knowing your mission, and ensuring that everything you do contributes to that mission

General Questions	- What is your "show"? What business are you really in? What is your mission?
- Look at the various activities you perform on a day-to-day basis. Do they all contribute to your "show"?
- Do you have a metaphor that communicates your mission like "show" does for Walt Disney Imagineering?
Game Design Questions	- What type of game am I designing?
Instructional Design Questions	- Are you effectively communicating ideas to your audience?
Management/ Leadership Questions	- What is is our mission? What do we do?

It All Begins with a Story

Using your subject matter to inform all decisions about your project

General Questions	<ul><li>What is your "story"?</li><li>What is your subject matter? What is your project about?</li><li>Are you basing decisions about your project on your subject matter?</li></ul>
Game Design Questions	<ul><li>What is your game about?</li><li>Have you evaluated the elements of your game to make sure they fit with your story?</li><li>How do you reinforce your game's story through your game's rules?</li></ul>
Instructional Design Questions	<ul><li>Do you keep your subject matter in mind when developing your content?</li><li>Have you excluded tangential topics where appropriate and/or necessary?</li></ul>
Management/ Leadership Questions	<ul><li>What is your specific domain and how does it relate to your project?</li><li>What are some of the specifics of the project you're working on?</li></ul>

Creative Intent

Staying focused on your objective

General Questions	- What is your objective? What is your creative intent? - What is the experience you want your audience to have? - As you evaluate decisions and next steps in the life of your project, ask yourself, "Does this help me move closer to achieving my objective?"
Game Design Questions	- What is your objective in designing your game? - What is the experience you want players of your game to have? - Does your game have specific mechanics-based objectives? - Does your game have a story-based or setting-based objective?
Instructional Design Questions	- Are you focusing on your target audience? - Do you evaluate how each element contributes to the overall goals of the course?
Management/ Leadership Questions	- Are you focusing on your target audience? - Do you evaluate how each element contributes to the overall goals of the course?

Attention to Detail

Paying attention to every detail

General Questions	• Are you paying attention to the details of your project? • Does this detail support your subject matter or story? • Does this detail support your creative intent? • Are you including too much detail? Too little?
Game Design Questions	• Are you taking care to use appropriate details in your explanations and examples? • How can you use specific types of details to influence your players as they play your game?
Instructional Design Questions	• Have you verified the details in your materials? • Are you including too much detail? Too little?
Management/ Leadership Questions	• Are you sharing appropriate details at the appropriate time? • What does the team need to know to complete each part of this project? • What does the team need to know to avoid challenges at later stages of the project?

Theming

Using appropriate details to strengthen your story and creative intent

General Questions	<ul><li>Are you using details that support your story, and don't distract your audience?</li><li>Are you being consistent in your use of language and terminology?</li><li>Are you being consistent in your use of templates and formatting?</li></ul>
Game Design Questions	<ul><li>Are you using graphic design elements that reinforce your game's subject matter or creative intent?</li><li>How do the various elements of your game reinforce its story?</li></ul>
Instructional Design Questions	<ul><li>Are you being consistent in your use of language and terminology?</li><li>Are you being consistent in your use of templates and formatting?</li></ul>
Management/ Leadership Questions	<ul><li>Are you consistent with your team?</li></ul>

Long, Medium, and Close Shots

Organizing your message to lead your audience from the general to the specific

General Questions	- What is your establishing shot? - What is your medium shot? - What is your close up? - How do your close-up details support your establishing shot?
Game Design Questions	- Are you using establishing shots to present information about your game to your players? - How are you providing your players with more information about your game and its setting?
Instructional Design Questions	- Have you identified your establishing (long) and close shots? - Are you presenting information in a way that moves from the general to the specific? - Are you using different levels of detail to help guide your audience through your material?
Management/ Leadership Questions	- Do you use establishing shots to help introduce new ideas? - If you've been forced to become a generalist (through promotions/ advancement), do you still take the time to focus on medium and close-up details with your team?

Wienies

Attracting your audience's attention and capturing their interest

General Questions	- What type of wienie makes sense for your project? Should you use visual wienies, verbal wienies, or both? - Are you using creative language to entice your audience to want to learn more about your project? - Are you using effective graphic design to capture your audience's attention and interest?
Game Design Questions	- Are you using wienies to capture your player's attention? - Can you use the Nintendo Effect in your game?
Instructional Design Questions	- Do you provide compelling reasons for students to participate? - Have you explained what skills your audience can expect to learn?
Management/ Leadership Questions	- Do you share goals with your team in a way that inspires them? - Are you using milestones or key deliverables as wienies?

Transitions

Making changes as smooth and seamless as possible

General Questions	<ul><li>Are there specific tools to help create effective transitions in your project?</li><li>Are you avoiding abrupt changes?</li><li>Are you guiding your audience from subject to subject in a manner that helps them understand?</li><li>Have you considered the order in which you're presenting your ideas? Do they flow smoothly from one to the next, or do they jump around?</li></ul>
Game Design Questions	<ul><li>How are you organizing the rules of your game?</li><li>Are the transitions between levels/areas of your game smooth or jagged?</li></ul>
Instructional Design Questions	<ul><li>Are you guiding your audience from subject to subject in a manner that helps them learn?</li><li>How can you avoid being tripped up by the Curse of Knowledge?</li><li>Have you identified areas where you need to differ from "real world practice" in order to clearly communicate to your audience?</li></ul>
Management/ Leadership Questions	<ul><li>How are you managing change in your organization?</li><li>Do you really understand the change that is taking place (What, Why, and How)?</li><li>How can you most effectively communicate change to your team?</li></ul>

Storyboards

Focusing on the big picture

General Questions	- Are using storyboards or a mind map to visualize your project? - Have you stepped back to "see" your entire project? - Have you considered different ways in which to arrange the pieces of your project?
Game Design Questions	- Are you using storyboards to plot out the story of your game? - How could you employ mind mapping or storyboard tools to help you organize your game rules or setting information?
Instructional Design Questions	- Have you outlined the entire classroom experience? - Have you stepped back to "see" the entire course? - Have you considered different ways to arrange the "events" of the course?
Management/ Leadership Questions	- Are you keeping the big picture in mind? - How do you communicate the bigger picture to your team?

Pre-Shows and Post-Shows

Introducing and reinforcing your story to help your audience get and stay engaged

General Questions	<ul><li>What is your pre-show? How are you introducing your subject matter to your audience?</li><li>Do you have a post-show? How are you reinforcing your subject matter for your audience?</li></ul>
Game Design Questions	<ul><li>Does your game use introductory scenes (or fiction) to help establish the setting?</li><li>Do you use cut scenes in your game?</li><li>How do you reinforce ideas to your players?</li></ul>
Instructional Design Questions	<ul><li>Do you outline your learning objectives?</li><li>Do you introduce your topics and how they relate to your subject matter and to other topics?</li><li>Do you reinforce your subject matter at the end of each lesson?</li></ul>
Management/ Leadership Questions	<ul><li>Do you have project kick-off meetings?</li><li>Do you have lessons-learned sessions after projects?</li></ul>

Forced Perspective
Using the illusion of size to help communicate your message

General Questions	<ul><li>Are you trying to adjust your audience's perspective to help communicate your message?</li><li>Are you simplifying large or complex subjects?</li><li>Are using grouping and/or chunking?</li><li>How can you employ Tolkien's distant mountains?</li></ul>
Game Design Questions	<ul><li>How can you make your game seem smaller or simpler than it is?</li><li>Does your game world include distant mountains?</li></ul>
Instructional Design Questions	<ul><li>Are you trying to adjust your audience's perspective to help them learn?</li><li>Are you simplifying large or complex subjects?</li></ul>
Management/ Leadership Questions	<ul><li>How can you "shrink" the size of your project?</li><li>Are you promoting your team's efforts in the right way?</li></ul>

"Read"-ability
Simplifying complex subjects

General Questions	▪ Are you simplifying complex ideas? ▪ How can you make your subject matter more "read"-able? ▪ Are you using illustrations, examples, or metaphors to help explain your subject matter?
Game Design Questions	▪ Can you use illustrations to simplify certain rules and mechanics? ▪ Could you use a metaphor or example to help explain the more abstract or difficult concepts in your game?
Instructional Design Questions	▪ Do you use examples, illustrations, or metaphors to help explain complex subjects? ▪ Are you using the six approaches to simplification from *The Art of Explanation* to help simplify your message?
Management/ Leadership Questions	▪ Are you simplifying your message? ▪ Are you using executive summaries or pitches when presenting your ideas?

Kinetics

Keeping the experience dynamic and active

General Questions	<ul><li>Is your project dynamic and active?</li><li>How can you make your project more dynamic and active?</li><li>How can you employ variety in your project?</li><li>How can you add movement and motion to your project?</li></ul>
Game Design Questions	<ul><li>How can you include dynamic and active gameplay elements?</li><li>Are you providing opportunities for interesting combinations of game elements in your game?</li><li>Could you include physical activity as part of your game?</li></ul>
Instructional Design Questions	<ul><li>Is your experience "active"?</li><li>Do you use hands-on exercises?</li><li>Have you developed demonstrations that illustrate course concepts?</li><li>Do you include quizzes, polling questions, or other interactive activities?</li></ul>
Management/ Leadership Questions	<ul><li>How can you assign different people to different tasks to keep your team active and engaged?</li><li>Are you looking for ways to assign different sets of people to work together?</li><li>Do you know the strengths and weaknesses of your co-workers?</li></ul>

The "it's a small world" Effect

Using repetition and reinforcement to make your audience's experience and your message memorable

General Questions	<ul><li>Are you reinforcing key ideas and concepts?</li><li>Are you using repetition to help reinforce ideas?</li><li>How can you employ other Imagineering practices to help reinforce your ideas?</li></ul>
Game Design Questions	<ul><li>Does your game incorporate repetition to help players improve their skills?</li><li>Are you reinforcing the key concepts of your game enough?</li></ul>
Instructional Design Questions	<ul><li>Are you reinforcing key ideas and concepts?</li><li>Are you using repetition to help reinforce ideas?</li><li>Are you using repetition to help reinforce ideas?</li></ul>
Management/ Leadership Questions	<ul><li>Are you employing repetition?</li><li>Are you employing repetition?</li><li>Are you consistently reminding your team about important goals and objectives?</li><li>Are you providing opportunities for your people to practice new skills?</li></ul>

Hidden Mickeys

Involving and engaging your audience

General Questions	▪ How are you engaging and involving your audience? ▪ Are you providing ways for your audience to figure some things out on their own? ▪ Do you ask questions that force your audience to think about your message and how it applies to them? ▪ Have you incorporated the equivalent of Hidden Mickeys or five-legged goats in your project?
Game Design Questions	▪ Does your game allow for players to devise their own strategies? ▪ Does your game include Easter eggs that players can discover as they play through the game? ▪ Does your game include emergent gameplay?
Instructional Design Questions	▪ Are you providing ways for students to figure some things out on their own? ▪ Do you ask questions that force students to think beyond the boundaries of your subject matter?
Management/ Leadership Questions	▪ Do the members of your team have hidden talents that you can help them develop? ▪ How can you learn more about your team members' interests both on and off the job?

Plussing

Consistently asking, "How Do I Make This Better?"

General Questions	<ul><li>How can you make your audience's experience better?</li><li>Do you have your own version of WDI's Show Quality Standards?</li><li>How can you apply other Imagineering Pyramid tools to your project to plus it?</li><li>What little things can you add or change in your project that might improve the experience for your audience?</li></ul>
Game Design Questions	<ul><li>Have you examined your game through the lens of Jesse Schell's eight filters?</li><li>How many times have you tested and iterated your design?</li><li>Have you playtested your game? Have you playtested your game enough?</li></ul>
Instructional Design Questions	<ul><li>How can you make your course better?</li><li>What little things can you add or change in your course that might improve the learning experience for your audience?</li></ul>
Management/ Leadership Questions	<ul><li>Are you using "lessons-learned" sessions to identify areas of improvement?</li><li>How can you and your team consistently focus on improvement?</li></ul>

Bibliography

Books

Baham, Jeff. *The Unauthorized Story of Walt Disney's Haunted Mansion.* Winter Garden: Theme Park Press, 2014.

Barnes, Jeffrey A. *The Wisdom of Walt: Leadership Lessons From the Happiest Place on Earth.* Lake Placid: Aviva Publishing, 2015.

Barrett, Steven M. *Hidden Mickeys: A Field Guide to Walt Disney World's Best Kept Secrets*, 4th Edition. Branford: The Intrepid Traveler, 2009.

Burkus, David. *The Myths of Creativity: The Truth About How Innovative Companies and People Generate Great Ideas.* San Francisco: Jossey-Bass, 2014.

Covey, Stephen R. *The 7 Habits of Highly Effective People: Restoring the Character Ethic.* New York: Fireside, 1990.

Covey, Stephen R. *Principle-Centered Leadership.* New York: Fireside, 1992.

Crump, Rolly. *More Cute Stories, Volume I: Disneyland History.* Baltimore: Bamboo Forest Publishing, 2014.

Crump, Rolly. *More Cute Stories, Volume 2: Animators and Imagineers.* Baltimore: Bamboo Forest Publishing, 2015.

Disney Imagineers, The. *The Imagineering Workout: Exercises to Shape Your Creative Muscles.* New York: Disney Editions, Inc., 2005.

Frederick, Matthew. *101 Things I Learned in Architecture School.* Cambridge: The MIT Press, 2007.

Geary, James. *I Is an Other: The Secret Life of Metaphor and How It Shapes the Way We See the World.* New York: Harper Collins Publishers, 2011.

Gennawey, Sam. *The Disneyland Story: The Unauthorized Guide to the Evolution of Walt Disney's Dream.* Birmingham: Keen Communications, LLC., 2014.

Grossman, Austin. *The Art of Epic Mickey.* New York: Disney Editions, Inc., 2011.

Handke, Danny and Hunt, Vanessa. *Poster Art of the Disney Parks.* New York: Disney Editions, Inc., 2012.

Heath, Chip and Dan Heath. *Made to Stick: Why Some Ideas Survive and Other Die.* New York: Random House, 2007.

Hench, John, and Peggy Van Pelt. *Designing Disney: Imagineering and the Art of the Show*. New York: Disney Editions, Inc., 1998.

Imagineers, The. *The Imagineering Way: Ideas to Ignite Your Creativity*. New York: Disney Editions, Inc., 2003.

Imagineers, The, and Kevin Rafferty. *Walt Disney Imagineering: A Behind the Dreams Look at Making the Magic Real*. New York: Hyperion, 1996.

Imagineers, The, and Melody Malmberg. *Walt Disney Imagineering: A Behind the Dreams Look at Making MORE Magic Real*. New York: Disney Editions, Inc., 2010.

Kelley, Tom and David Kelley. *Creative Confidence: Unleashing the Creative Potential Within Us All*. New York: Crown Business, 2013.

Korkis, Jim. *Who's the Leader of the Club: Walt Disney's Leadership Lessons*. Winter Garden: Theme Park Press, 2014.

Kurti, Jeff. *Walt Disney's Imagineering Legends and the Genesis of the Disney Theme Park*. New York: Disney Editions, Inc., 2008.

Landau, Neil. *101 Things I Learned in Film School*. New York: Grand Central Publishing, 2010.

Lefever, Lee. *The Art of Explanation: Making Your Ideas, Products, and Services Easier to Understand*. Hoboken: John Wiley & Sons, Inc., 2013.

Leffkon, Wendy (editorial director). *Marc Davis: Walt Disney's Renaissance Man*. Glendale: Disney Editions, Inc., 2014.

Littaye, Alain and Didier Ghez. *Disneyland Paris: From Sketch to Reality*. London: Neverland Editions, 2013.

MacKenzie, Gordon. *Orbiting the Giant Hairball: A Corporate Fool's Guide to Surviving with Grace*. New York: Penguin Putnam, 1996.

May, Matthew E. *In Pursuit of Elegance: Why the Best Ideas Have Something Missing*. New York: Broadway Books, 2009.

McGonigal, Jane. *Reality is Broken: Why Games Make Us Better and How They Can Change the World*. New York: The Penguin Press, 2011.

Pink, Daniel H. *To Sell Is Human: The Surprising Truth About Moving Others*. New York: Riverhead Books, 2012.

Preis, Michael W. *101 Things I Learned in Business School*. New York: Grand Central Publishing, 2010.

Robbins, Anthony. *Awaken The Giant Within: How to Take Immediate Control of Your Mental, Emotional, Physical, and Financial Destiny*. New York: Summit Books, 1991.

Schell, Jesse. *The Art of Game Design: A Book of Lenses*. Burlington: Morgan Kaufmann Publishers, 2008.

Sims, Peter. *Little Bets: How Breakthrough Ideas Emerge from Small Discoveries*. New York: Free Press, 2011.

Sklar, Marty. *One Little Spark: Mickey's Ten Commandments and The Road to Imagineering*. Glendale: Disney Editions, Inc. 2015

Surrell, Jason. *The Haunted Mansion: From the Magic Kingdom to the Movies*. New York: Disney Editions, Inc., 2003.

Surrell, Jason. *Pirates of the Caribbean: From the Magic Kingdom to the Movies*. New York: Disney Editions, Inc., 2005.

Surrell, Jason. *The Disney Mountains: Imagineering at Its Peak*. New York: Disney Editions, Inc., 2007.

Tharp, Twyla. *The Creative Habit: Learn It and Use It for Life*. New York: Simon & Schuster Paperbacks, 2003.

Williams, Pat, and Jim Denney. *How To Be Like Walt: Capturing the Disney Magic Every Day of Your Life*. Deerfield Beach: Health Communications, Inc., 2004.

Wooden, John, and Steve Jamison. *Wooden: A Lifetime of Observations and Reflections On and Off the Court*. Chicago: Contemporary Books, 1997.

Wright, Alex. *The Imagineering Field Guide to the Magic Kingdom at Walt Disney World*. New York: Disney Editions, Inc., 2005.

Wright, Alex. *The Imagineering Field Guide to Epcot at Walt Disney World*. New York: Disney Editions, Inc., 2006.

Wright, Alex. *The Imagineering Field Guide to Disney's Animal Kingdom Theme Park at Walt Disney World*. New York: Disney Editions, Inc., 2007.

Wright, Alex. *The Imagineering Field Guide to Disneyland*. New York: Disney Editions, Inc., 2008.

Wright, Alex. *The Imagineering Field Guide to Disney's Hollywood Studios at Walt Disney World*. New York: Disney Editions, Inc., 2010.

Wright, Alex. *The Imagineering Field Guide to Disney California Adventure at Disneyland Resort*. New York: Disney Editions, Inc., 2014.

Magazine Articles

"Disney's Space Mountain." *The "E" Ticket*, Number 30, Fall 1998

"Pirates of the Caribbean...More Gems from This Disney Treasure" *The "E" Ticket*, Number 32, Fall 1999.

"The Hatbox Ghost." *The "E" Ticket*, Number 32, Fall 1999.

Acknowledgments

Though I may been the one who did the actual writing, this book was not truly a solo effort. I have many people to thank who helped me make it a reality. My sincere thanks go out to the following:

- My wife, Sheri, and my kids, Nathan and Samantha, for their unconditional love and support. I wouldn't be who I am without them. I love them all more than words can truly express.

- My family and friends for their continued support, encouragement, and enthusiasm throughout this process. It's amazing what an occasional "How's your book going?" or "Hey, I heard you're writing a book" can do for your morale.

- John Fox at the Society of Applied Learning Technology (SALT) for giving me the first opportunity to share these ideas with an audience at the SALT Conference in Orlando in February 2011.

- Bob McLain at Theme Park Press for giving me the chance to expand my ideas about the Imagineering Pyramid into this book and share them with a larger audience.

- Tania Helhoski at BirdDesign, for the Imagineering Pyramid diagrams in this book.

- Jeff Barnes, David Burkus, Rolly Crump, Sean Patrick Fannon, Sam Gennawey, Greg Gorden, Robin Laws, Louis Lemoine, Sam Lewis, Dan Pink, Warren Spector, Jason Surrell, and C. McNair Wilson for reading an early draft of this book and providing helpful comments, feedback, and endorsements.

- Steven M. Barret and Jeff Lange, for the use of their photos in the Hidden Mickeys chapter.

- Imagineer Jason Grandt, for the wonderful and engaging stories he shared with my family and I during our "lunch with an Imagineer" in August 2010, for talking about Imagineering with me over dinner at Ragland Road in February 2011, and for putting up with all of my questions.

- Imagineer Alex Wright, for answering questions about Imagineering and the *Imagineering Field Guide* series.
- Lastly, everyone who I have ever visited a Disney theme park with—including family, friends, and the faculty, students, and chaperones of the 2012–2013 Wakefield High School Music Department—for helping me see the Disney parks through different eyes each time I visit.

About the Imagineering Toolbox Series

This book is the first in the Imagineering Toolbox series. The Imagineering Toolbox is a collection of tools inspired by Walt Disney Imagineering, the division of The Walt Disney Company responsible for the design and development of Disney theme parks, resorts, cruise ships, shopping areas, and other venues and attractions.

The Imagineering Pyramid is one set of the tools found in the Imagineering Toolbox, comprising 15 practices and principles used by Walt Disney Imagineering in the design and construction of Disney theme parks.

The next book in the series will focus on the process the Imagineers use to design and build Disney theme park attractions, resorts, and other venues. *The Imagineering Process* is a simplified version of the process Walt Disney Imagineering uses and can serve as a model for designing and creating nearly any type of creative project.

About the Author

Lou Prosperi spent 10 years working in the game industry as a freelance game designer and writer, as well as a product line developer at FASA Corporation, where he worked on the *Earthdawn* roleplaying game. After leaving FASA Corporation, Lou went to work as a technical writer and instructional designer and has been in that role for the last 15 years, writing user and technical documentation and training materials for enterprise software applications. He currently manages a small team of technical writers and curriculum developers for a small business unit of a large enterprise software company.

Lou has been interested in (or obsessed with, depending on who you ask) Disney parks since his first visit to Walt Disney World on his honeymoon in 1993. A self-described "student of Imagineering", Lou has been collecting books about the Disney company, Disney parks, and Imagineering for the last 10+ years. Lou rarely passes up an opportunity to add new books to his Disney and Imagineering libraries, and is nearly always thinking about his next trip to Walt Disney World. He lives in Wakefield, Massachusetts, with his wife and children.

You can contact Lou via email or on social media at the following:

- *Email* LJP1963@aol.com
- *Facebook* facebook.com/lou.prosperi
- *Twitter* twitter.com/louprosperi
- *Pinterest* pinterest.com/louprosperi
- *Academia* roosevelt.academia.edu/LouProsperi

More Books from Theme Park Press

Theme Park Press publishes dozens of books each year for Disney fans and for general and academic audiences. Here are just a few of our titles. For the complete catalog, including book descriptions and excerpts, please visit:

ThemeParkPress.com

INSIDE THE DISNEY MARKETING MACHINE

In the Era of Michael Eisner & Frank Wells

Lorraine Santoli

Foreword by Sam Tuchman, Ph.D.

Walt Disney AND THE PROMISE OF Progress City

SAM GENNAWEY

Foreword by Werner Weiss

MOUSE IN TRANSITION

An Insider's Look at Disney Feature Animation

STEVE HULETT

Foreword by John Musker
Disney Feature Films Animation Director

DISNEY'S HOLLYWOOD STUDIOS

FROM SHOW BIZ TO YOUR BIZ

J. JEFF KOBER

Great Big Beautiful Tomorrow

Walt Disney and Technology

Christian Moran
with Rolly Crump,
Bob Gurr, Jim Korkis,
Sam Gennawey, and Dr.
Maureen Furniss, Ph.D.

DISNEY BY THE NUMBERS

FACTS AND FIGURES ABOUT
THE WALT DISNEY WORLD
THEME PARKS AND
RESORTS

ANTHONY M. CASELNOVA

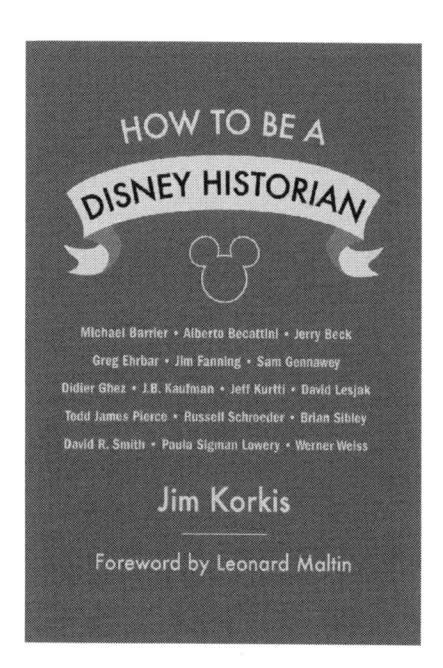

HOW TO BE A DISNEY HISTORIAN

Michael Barrier • Alberto Becattini • Jerry Beck
Greg Ehrbar • Jim Fanning • Sam Gennawey
Didier Ghez • J.B. Kaufman • Jeff Kurtti • David Lesjak
Todd James Pierce • Russell Schroeder • Brian Sibley
David R. Smith • Paula Sigman Lowery • Werner Weiss

Jim Korkis

Foreword by Leonard Maltin

DISNEY'S GRAND TOUR

WALT AND ROY'S EUROPEAN VACATION
SUMMER 1935

DIDIER GHEZ

From Disneyland's Tom Sawyer to Disney Legend
The Adventures of Tom Nabbe
TOM NABBE

From Jungle Cruise Skipper to Disney Legend
40 Years of Magical Memories at Disney
William "Sully" Sullivan

A Historical Tour of Walt Disney World
- Jungle Cruise
- Enchanted Tiki Room
- Carousel of Progress
- Pirates of the Caribbean
- Crystal Palace
- Tomorrowland

Main Street, U.S.A.

VOLUME I

ANDREW KISTE

WINDOW ON MAIN STREET
35 Years of Creating Happiness at Disneyland Park

Van Arsdale France
Founder
and
Professor Emeritus
Disney Universities

Van Arsdale France
Foreword by Dick Nunis
Former Chairman, Walt Disney Attractions

Printed in Great Britain
by Amazon